TOURING
LONDON

"THE CITY"

Looking toward St. Paul's Cathedral

Touring London

with

W. TEIGNMOUTH SHORE

A little book of friendly guidance for
THOSE WHO VISIT LONDON &
THOSE WHO DWELL IN LONDON

With an Introductory Note by
The Rt. Hon. JOHN BURNS, P.C.

Illustrated

NEW YORK
CHARLES SCRIBNER'S SONS
LONDON B.T. BATSFORD LTD
1930

First Published, Spring 1930

MADE AND PRINTED IN GREAT BRITAIN
BY THE STANHOPE PRESS, ROCHESTER
FOR B. T. BATSFORD, LIMITED, LONDON

INTRODUCTORY NOTE

By the Rt. Hon. JOHN BURNS

*London is so old, so vast, so complex and kaleidoscopic
in variety and changes that it is difficult so to describe
it as to make the description a verbal or pictorial micro-
cosm of the metropolis. Its history is a continuing
palimpsest on which is superimposed too prominently the
life of the later periods, to the detriment of the earlier
and formative time, too often forgotten by the present
generation in these fretful and forgetful days.*

*I believe London always was a world magnet, as west-
ward Eastern peoples always made their venturing and
wandering way. Its insular character always appealed
to the Continental peoples from Ancient Greece to
modern Germany. Its central position in the maritime
world lured the mariner, stimulated the merchant and
excited the ambitious. Its great antiquity and its con-
tinuous worth and wealth evoke the respect which is due
to a community to which the words of Pliny would now
apply "Have reverence for ancient glory, old age vener-
able in a man is sacred in a city."*

*And in 1501, Sir William Dunbar called London "the
flour of Cities all." Later John Milton called it the
"Mansion House of Liberty." This praise of London
can truthfully be applied to London, because in all its
periods, its people have shown industrial skill, martial*

vii

*valour, naval courage, political sagacity and have pro-
duced, reared or stimulated nearly all the greatest men
of Britain's Isle. The greatest of the provincials have
been influenced by its urbanity, inspired by its associations,
elevated by its traditions, and their potentials have been
exalted by its corporate impulse. Britain's greatest men
born away from London have added to their literary,
dramatic, and poetical stature by their contact with
London. Shakespeare, Johnson, Goldsmith, Garrick,
masters of their craft, found in London the larger atmosphere, the greater stage and the wider outlook for
their genius, the medium for its expression and the
reward for their labours. All poets, artists, actors,
singers and writers look to London as the Mecca of their
ambition and their crown of recognition, and crave, and
esteem, and hopefully expect and finally secure the
critical yet kindly verdict and hallmark of Londoners'
approval.*

*From Shakespeare to Shaw the praise of London is
higher than the Hochs of Berlin, the Vivas of Rome, or
the frenzied but transient applause of Paris. This
London quality of distinctive impartiality is the gregarious
inheritance of centuries of civic association, habit,
training, and the corporate instinct that through long
periods have made London the arbiter of England's social
and political life. London is the social crucible in which
the best elements of a Commonwealth, through the experience
of a highly organised city, have been compounded in their
right proportions by persistent trial and experiment.*

*London has always been anti-clerical, pro Parliament;
always rebellious, when class becoming caste has pressed
the populace too far, and provoked the responsible
citizens with sectional aims and individual exactions.
Our great parks and gardens testify to the victories of the
common people in resisting in the metropolis the im-*

viii

*plications of rural enclosures which made a bold
peasantry in the country-side a landless people.*

*The hillocks of the corner of the Green Park, where grazing
sheep can often be seen, testify 300 years after how London
men, women and children threw up elevated forts to
resist Charles I's march from Oxford to London, as
humorously testified to by Hudibras. The Common
Council by Order called upon the ministers of religion to
stir up the Parishioners in their parishes to send such of
their servants and children as were fit to labour with
spades and shovels to the raising of outworks for the
defence of the City. The very women helped in this
work, titled ladies showing great activity. Butler in*
Hudibras *tells us how the women laboured. What
have they done or what left undone that might advance
the cause of London :*

> *"March, rank and file with drum and ensign*
> *T' entrench the City for defence in;*
> *Raised Rampiers with their own soft hands*
> *To put the Enemy to stands*
> *From Ladies down to oyster Wenches*
> *Labour'd like Pioneers in Trenches*
> *Fall'n to their pickaxes and tools*
> *And help'd the men to dig like moles."*

*London being a real metropolis, on a matchless river
with a peerless port, is also a Capital city by having a
national Parliament within its boundaries. The combination of these unique conditions has led to the acquisi-
tion by the common people of large instalments of liberty
and freedom. The success thereby of popular institutions
has created a spirit, temper and conduct of and by the
citizens themselves that in other cities is imposed upon
them. The pride of citizenship, that comes from use of
power, and the right to maintain popular rights with
individual duties blended in Londoners as nowhere else.*

ix

Their motto might be as their conduct generally is, so to comport themselves as men as not to forget they are citizens, and to the strangers in the streets this quality is responsible for the universal courtesy the Cockney displays to the visitors from all countries. But the great appeal London makes to all provincials and the foreigner is the vastness, variety and rarity of its treasures. As the best exposition of universal art the National Gallery leads the world in the excellence and condition of its pictures.

The British Museum, the greatest of all libraries, the 700 other libraries with 1,200 collections are available as nowhere else to all students. The Tower of London, with its picturesque and grisly history, in a histrionic setting is the best ancient building of its type. Hampton Court on an English summer day is the greatest pleasaunce I know. A marvellous combination of good and epochal architecture on a pleasant river with ancient trees, splendid turf, beautiful flowers, with great masses of grass and shrubbery and a freedom of movement and access equal to its total charm.

A feature of London life as distinctive as it is agreeable is the important social and hygienic fact that London is still a city of small houses, and has in proportion to its numbers and area the largest number of Parks, Gardens, Squares and Playgrounds of all the great cities. Not being a conscript people, a tariff-ridden community or a protected country, it is not numbered, registered, regimented and quartered in barrack dwellings.

Someone said that every Englishman was an Island and every English house was a castle. Less true than years ago these characteristics have good qualities and differentiate London from other cities. The Londoner is not a "Boulevardier" and never will be. Climate, custom, temper, disposition, character, personality have and will

x

prevent this undesirable end. His reserve often runs into snobbery, but take the Londoner all through he is a courteous, kindly, good-natured person.

The matchless and increasing greenery of London's parks and gardens, 1,000 in number, 33,000 acres and 10 per cent. of its total area, surprises even the countrymen from places where every prospect pleases but only man is railed.

A rich American, a dependent beggar with a million bits of gold, once dwelt in a West End club. Midas-like he found that gold was not digestible and he wanted other things. Being thrifty by accumulating other peoples' money he sought in London the endless ways of cheap entertainment. He hired one room, his maintenance was about the yearly cost of a London policeman and he averred that his tastes were simple because his elder wants were few. He asked for nothing more than to walk from his club eastward to St. Martin's Church, see the National Gallery, feed the Trafalgar Square pigeons, hear the best music of the Guards' Band at St. James's Palace, watch the colour and bravery of the attendant Life Guards, walk round St. James's Park and so to lunch, and with a delight worthy of the following vagrant, assure us that he was the heir of all the ages for nothing until he was gathered to his fathers.

Last but not least, the most enduring and valuable of all London's attractions is its wonderful river. The greatest boon that city ever had, its wealth, health, movement and security are endeared to artist, trader, sailor and tourist.

Well equipped, generously maintained, humanely administered, all London's social and municipal services are increasingly the models for other communities, the lengthening life of its people, its great water supply, its wonderful health, the multifold attractions to no small extent account for its expansion, and in my judgment, if not checked, may add to its risks and dangers.

If we are to judge the London of the present by the past and both as a guide or portent for the future, we of the 20th century will not fail for lack of information. Books large and small in size, great and little in their conception of London, are always being written and, I trust, read as much by citizens as tourists. The idealist who is above and who sees beyond mere size, numbers, wealth and expansion of cities, can visualise London as More saw it as the Utopia of his ideals.

He can share with Blake his fancy of

> *"The fields of Islington to Marybone,*
> *To Primrose Hill and St. Johns Wood,*
> *Were builded over with pillars of gold*
> *And there Jerusalem pillars stood."*

The lover of London who has written this book, Teignmouth Shore, has taken pains to picture its places and describe worthily many of the chief features of its romantic history and places of interest. He is an authority on London and the proof of his knowledge is contained in this, one of the most suitable and practical guides to this great and fascinating yet neighbourly city. I heartily commend it.

The publishers are much indebted to the
following for their generous help in granting
permission to use the drawings and photographs
with which this work is illustrated:—

Sir Banister Fletcher, P.R.I.B.A., Fig. 2,
from "A History of Architecture"; Mr. H. N.
King, Plates VII₂ and VIII₁; London Elec-
tric Railways, Figs. 11 and 15 from "London
Town and Country"; Mr. A. E. Payne, Plate
XIV; Mr. Roland W. Paul, F.S.A., Figs. 1
and 9, from "Vanishing London"; Sir Andrew
T. Taylor, F.S.A. for figures reproduced from
"The Towers and Steeples designed by Sir
Christopher Wren"; Mr. Will F. Taylor, Plates
XII₂, XIV₂, II; Mr. Edward Yates, Plate VIII²;
and Mr. Br¹an C. Cook for the map at end.

AUTHOR'S NOTE

There are unusually wide margins to this little book. Not in order to make it look big or pretty, but for this practical purpose. It is useful and pleasant to be able to make marginal notes in a guidebook, is it not? I think so and I do so; therefore, I feel it friendly to provide room for you to do so.

CONTENTS

"London, thou art the Flour of Cities all."

William Dunbar

"In London I never knew what I'd be at,
Enraptured with this, and enchanted with that."

Charles Morris

"Dear, damn'd, distracting town."   *Alexander Pope*

INTRODUCTION

"And the green country meadows
Are fresh and fine to see,
But the grey streets of London
They're all the world to me."

Rosamund Marriott Watson

THIS is my introduction to you, as one willing and, I hope, able to take you about the town that I have loved and studied for many years. I am not making any attempt to provide you with a guide-book, but only with a guide, talking with you, as it were, as I have done with many friends who have visited London and who could not spend many days in exploring or hope to visit all the "sights." But I trust that my conversation may provide matter of interest to the Londoner as well as to the visitor, and that, although he—or she—may not desire to follow me in detail on any of the Tours, without some individual variation, he may find here and there a finger-post directing him to some quarter of the town hitherto unexplored or with which he is imperfectly acquainted. Indeed, to the question "Do you know *your* London?" are there many citizens who can truthfully respond with a plump "Yes, I do."

London is so vast and varied that to the hasty visitor it usually seems to lack personality. London has a soul and an individuality; but its great heart is not easily won. Even those who have lived there a long life-time often feel that they are strangers in a strange place, of which they have seen much but know not much. How then can a passing guest be able to become friendly and intimate with it? Only, I think, by talking with one who is London's familiar comrade.

LOOK AT YOUR MAP

The first feeling that must assail a visitor to London, especially one who comes from over-seas, is bewilderment. There seems to be no key to this aimless welter of streets, apparently laid out without design or forethought. London was not planned. It has grown, almost haphazard.

The "river," the Thames, upon which few Londoners have been and which many have never seen, was for hundreds of years the main thoroughfare. Look at your map! The river is still the main artery of London, though no longer its carrier of passenger traffic. When the City broke its bounds and the Town crept over the countryside, East, West, North, South, up hill and down dale, the river gradually lost its importance to the town traveller.

Look at your map! Actually take your place or imagine that you have done so in Trafalgar Square, which for the visitor is a most helpful and convenient centre of activities. You will see that London has many main routes of traffic going East and West, and others running North and South. Get the most important of these firm-fixed in your eye and London will no longer be a muddlesome place to you. Down in the South East corner of the Square is the opening of the Strand, which street was once simply the way along the river bank.

Following the Strand we reach Fleet Street, so called because it led down to the Fleet River, which now runs underground as a sewer to the river. On up Ludgate Hill, along Cannon Street, Queen Victoria Street, and so to the Bank and the Mansion House, the business and civic centres of the City proper. We will go back West—on our map—along Cheapside, which ages ago was the open market or chepe of London City, along Holborn, where the viaduct crosses the valley of the Fleet, Oxford Street, Bayswater and the Uxbridge roads, and so out into the country, if we keep on long enough!

Returning to Trafalgar Square: South run Whitehall and Parliament Street to Westminster. Pall Mall East leads to the Haymarket, and so to another convenient centre, Piccadilly Circus, the hub of fashionable, frivolous, luxury-loving London. Directly West runs famous Piccadilly; so along to Knightsbridge and Kensington. From Piccadilly Circus Northwards runs Regent Street, across Oxford Street, and so to Regent's Park, where are the Zoological Gardens, and eventually to Hampstead along the long Finchley Road.

This map-view of the main thoroughfares will enable you to fix your bearings and find your way about.

Of almost all the streets I have mentioned the names have historical meanings and origins; to a great extent the history of London is written in its street names. In the older parts of London the run of most of the main streets was dictated by the lie of the land and the run of rivers and streams. That London grew and was not laid out is the base of much of its beauty. Some parts of London

3

have a singular and penetrating beauty; much of it is ugly, but the discriminating visitor need not see this.

The multitudinous Squares are a London feature and are to be found in all quarters, and in the poorer districts they seem to have an added attraction. Groups and streets of Georgian and Queen Anne houses are to be seen in Westminster, Chelsea, Hampstead, Kensington and farther out. There is more of Shakespeare's London than even most Londoners know. There are Norman and mediæval churches. There are—well, we shall see. Londoners may think that they possess a fair or a full knowledge of their city and "know their way about." But there are curious, historic, and beautiful spots, nooks and corners hidden away behind even the most commercialised high thoroughfare; there are few main streets so prosaic that they do not mask a hinterland of romantic interest. I hope you, fellow cit, have cultivated the habit of rambling exploration; you are bound to find all sorts of pleasant surprises and interests, even an occasional discovery!

OUR TOURS

The four tours I have planned are little more than indicators of how to see a great deal in a short time and without undue rushing. You are not compelled to follow them exactly, you can compress or expand them; if you are wise, you can take each of them leisurely, which will mean devoting more than a day to each, re-planning with the aid of your map to suit your convenience, your tastes and your pocket-book. Following these routes you will not see all London. No man or woman has

done or could do that in however long a life-time.
But, if you keep your eyes open, your mind awake,
and will listen to what I have to say, you will
acquire a considerable knowledge of the town and
come into close touch with its personality. Nor will
you be able to see everything on each route; you
will have to pick and choose from that to which I
direct you. When my information is not sufficient,
there are many admirable guide-books, which will
aid you. Although I am an old Londoner, I find
my London Guides very charming companions.

GETTING ABOUT

The means of getting about London are much the
same as in other great cities. There is the main
choice of feet or wheels. By far the most pleasant
and most profitable way to travel London is to
walk it, in company of a friend who knows his way
about. But this is for the leisurely and the leisured.
The means of conveyance which will suit you
best is dependent upon your pocket-book and your
credit at the bank. If you have your own car, no
more need be said; you are able to go when and
where you will. Next best is to hire a taxi-cab
which will probably work out less costly than
hiring a car from or through your hotel. You
will be taken along your route and not driven
too fast, if you admonish the driver, to see things
as you go along. When you arrive at any place
where you desire to make a prolonged stay,
dismiss him with your blessing and his fare. With
very few exceptions you will find the driver
pleasant and obliging; he will take an interest
in you and will often be full of curious information which he will be ready to impart. You

5

must make him understand where you desire to go and what to see.

There are the Underground and "Tube" railways, omnibuses and street cars, commonly known as trams. For long distances the railways are quick and convenient, but their scenery is monotonous! They run East and West, North and South, with the Metropolitan Inner Circle as a big hoop, affording helpful "connections." The omnibus services are excellent, covering every point of importance in the City, the Town and the suburbs; but be sure you get the right bus and go in the right direction. Ask the "conductor." From the top of an omnibus London life can be well and amusingly seen; for those with limited purses it is the most economical way of getting around. Very useful and clear pocket maps are issued free, showing the bus, tram and underground routes in and near-by London. These can be obtained on the vehicle and at any Tube or Underground station. There are four of them: one for the buses, another for Tube trains, and another for trams, the fourth showing how to reach the country-side. These small guides supply a considerable amount of general information that is helpful to town travellers. With these and the maps in this volume you should not have any great difficulty in finding your way about. If you should ever lose your way—ask a policeman. The London "bobby" is a fine friend in need.

SHOPPING

It is very pleasant on a fine day to saunter, peering into shop windows, rejoicing in beautiful things that never can be mine and admiring what I cannot afford to purchase; it is an innocent and a cheap amusement. Although I do sometimes fall to temptations which I should resist! Often I find entertainment in the smaller shops and streets, but this is scarcely available to the stranger. The main shopping streets are round about Piccadilly Circus: namely Regent Street, Bond Street, Oxford Street, Piccadilly, Saint James's Street, the Haymarket, to name a few. This quarter has changed very greatly during the last few years, almost the whole of Regent Street and a considerable part of Piccadilly having been rebuilt; so that hereabouts much of the personality of London has departed, being replaced by a cosmopolitanism which may be convenient and sumptuous, but which is not always comely. Likewise the personality of the shops and stores themselves is vanishing, an uninteresting and unpersuasive sameness pervading most of the larger establishments. Those mentioned are not the only good shopping centres: there are the Strand, Cheapside and parts of Holborn; Westward there are Brompton Road, Sloane Street and Kensington High Street. As to how to shop, every woman knows and most men do not care.

AMUSEMENTS

The amusements of London are much of a muchness with those of other big cities. At many of the larger hotels and restaurants there are cabaret shows and dancing. Theatrical entertainments are plentiful, something to suit every liking. In May and June there is very grand opera at Covent Garden at very grand prices. Drury Lane has a great history, rather blurred by structural alterations and by the majority of recent productions. At the Haymarket Theatre will generally be found a good comedy and always fine acting. For the rest the play is the thing at each theatre, and you can make your choice of musical shows, melodramas, comedies, farces: occasionally a new piece by a famous writer or the revival of an old one by a dead-and-goner. For music, consult the papers and your desires.

The old-fashioned music-hall, with red nosed comedians, female male-impersonators, acrobats and so on, is nearly defunct; but a good variety show will usually be found at the Coliseum in Saint Martin's Lane off Trafalgar Square; at the Palladium close to Oxford Circus; or farther afield at the Holborn Empire and the Victoria Palace hard by Victoria Station. Queen Victoria did indeed make her mark!

MONEY

English money is not quite easy to those who meet it for the first time, though it is not more difficult to spend than is any other. A shilling is the best fixed point from which to calculate, up and down, being near enough the equivalent of a "quarter" dollar, U.S.A. Your calculations will be sufficiently accurate for everyday transactions, but if you are purchasing an automobile, an hotel, or jewellery for your wife, then you had best go to your banker, the American Exchange or to any of Cook's tourist offices to ascertain the day's rate of exchange.

EATING AND DRINKING

Man cannot live by sightseeing alone. If you are stopping at a boarding-house the question of mealing is pretty well decided for you, but when at an hotel you can dine out and about, with satisfaction and amusement. I will give only a few hints as to where and how, eating and drinking being so much matters of personal preference. Dining is a serious affair; it has been truly said that "a wasted appetite is a tragedy." Dinner, like so many nice things, has to be considered from the two points of view, "What I desire and what I can afford," the latter, alas, not always being in accord with the former. But discretion is the better part of expenditure, as of eating and drinking. There are restaurants of every class and quality in London, and you can feed yourself with the cookery of almost every country, including America.

While I think of it, here is a tip: at swagger restaurants you must tip the waiter to the tune of two shillings and sixpence per head of your party, as a minimum; at humbler places sixpence will do. But much depends upon the total of the bill and the amount of service asked for and received.

English cookery at its best is very, very good. You do not know what meat means until you have had a cut off a really-roast, not baked, sirloin of English beef or a slice from a saddle of English mutton. There are fairly good grills at most of the first-class hotels and restaurants, but a speciality is made of English fare at Simpson's in the Strand, where men alone should dine downstairs; and the fish joints there are excellent. Scott's in Coventry Street, facing down the Haymarket, is rightly noted for its fish, cooked and uncooked.

If you are a millionaire, or thereabouts, advice as to where to eat is uncalled for—the best is at your command. But if you are modestly endowed with pocket-money you can fare admirably at the following, among others: the Criterion, in Piccadilly Circus; the Trocadero and the Monico, at the lower end of Shaftesbury Avenue; Jules, in Jermyn Street; Romano's, in the Strand; Kettner's, in Church Street, Soho; Frascati, in Oxford Street. It may be taken as a golden rule, wherever you go, always choose dishes that must be prepared and cooked for *you*. That is why it is well to avoid *table d'hôte* meals. But if, like myself, you would dine still more modestly, but just as well (and sometimes better if you choose your dishes with discretion), usually with much more fun and generally without music, there are many small and unpretentious places that will serve your turn. Many of these are in that curious quarter of London called Soho, which lies South of Oxford Street, North of Leicester Square, West of Charing Cross Road, and East of Regent Street. It is a district of mingled gloom and light, wealth and sordid poverty; of fine houses, once the homes of fashion and beauty, if not always of virtue, now mostly gone to seed; broad ways and narrow; shops with foreign names and foreign goods. But its chief attraction is the number of small restaurants, where the cooking is mostly Italian and French, and often really admirable, and where the wines are reasonably cheap if not always coming from the country of their ostensible origin or having been born in the years that appear upon the label. The prices are on the whole very moderate, in some cases surprisingly so. I have eaten there, before the War, *table d'hôte* dinner of six courses, at the cost of a *shilling;* but as my appetite for supper afterward was urgent, my economy was false. It would be useless to give a long list of these places, so I will say no more than this: I have enjoyed excellent food at the *Italie*, in Greek Street, and at *l'Escargot*, almost immediately opposite; at the *Petit Riche*, in Old Compton Street. I do not for a moment mean that there are not other places equally admirable; but it is fair both to you and to myself to confine my recommendations to places with which I am familiar. As to the choice of wine, at an Italian house drink the wine of Italy, at a French that of France. Usually the very cheapest on the list is trustworthy, sound and at least palatable, being patronised by regular customers, who must be kept in good humour. The higher priced "vintages" are often should-be-goods. The so-called "special" coffee is seldom any better than the ordinary, and you can get a quite decent brandy for a couple of shillings. Warning; at any rate with ladies do not patronise a Chinese or other Oriental restaurant, without first assuring yourself that it is reputable.

So much, or rather so little, as to where to eat and drink, except for a few bits of advice I may give you when we are Touring.

OUTSIDE TOWN

My Tours will not carry you outside the town, because if I began to do that I should eventually find myself stepping off the island. There are many near-by places which should be visited, leisurely, by those who have time to do so. Kew, with its perfectly lovely gardens; Hampton Court, that incomparable Tudor palace, paraded by the ghosts of fat and furious Henry VIII and of many famous ladies of sunny faces and shady repute; Rochester, redolent of Dickens, Pickwick and Company, with Gad's Hill close by with more of Dickens and something of Jack Falstaff; thence, if time serves, on to glorious Canterbury; Windsor and Eton; Jordans, where Penn is buried with his two wives and five of his children; and, of course, Oxford.

FIRST TOUR

ROUTE: Trafalgar Square; the Strand; Fleet Street; Ludgate Hill; Saint Paul's Cathedral; the Mansion House and Roundabout; Cheapside; Newgate Street; Holborn; Oxford Street; Park Lane; Green Park; Saint James's Park; Trafalgar Square.

TRAFALGAR SQUARE is one of the most beautiful and historically interesting places in London. Go to the North side, standing against the stone parapet, overlooking the fountains and with your back turned to the National Gallery; and look around. About the National Gallery I will leave you to find out what you will, by visiting it some other day to see one of the finest collections of pictures in the world. I wonder will they have picture galleries in Heaven? Perhaps I shall not be given a chance of learning.

The Square itself dates from round about 1829, when it was laid out on the site of the Royal Mews. "All the King's horses," or most of them, are now in residence at Buckingham Palace; but, alas, the coming of the car has put the gee-gees' noses out of joint.

The tall pillar in front of you is the Nelson Monument, which the guide books tell us is 184 feet and 11 inches high, including the statue, which must feel a bit undignified being mast-headed like this.

Perhaps he climbs down at night to stretch his legs, possibly paying a visit to the Admiralty close by and expressing his opinion on naval developments since his time.

The church on your left hand is Saint Martin's-in-the-Fields, which it once actually was, when hereabouts it was mostly country-side, fields and lanes, green grass and flowers. At the font in this church were baptised Francis Bacon, John Hampden, Charles II and other worthies and unworthies. In the burial register you can see the names of Nell Gwynne, the pretty light-o-love of the above mentioned Charles, of Roubiliac, the sculptor, and of Thomas Chippendale, maker of chairs and tables. If you should chance to be without the price of a bed for the night, you will find the crypt here open as a night shelter for the homeless.

We will not bother about the various Colonial offices and so forth to the right and the left, but look straight ahead, almost due South-West, where you will see the opening of Whitehall, leading to Westminster; in the distance are the tall towers of the Houses of Parliament. On the left-hand side of Whitehall is the building from which Charles I stepped out onto the scaffold. Facing down this famous way is his statue (PLATE II), set up here in 1674, on the site of Charing Cross, which had been put here in 1294 to mark for ever the last halting-place on the road to Westminster Abbey of the funeral procession of Eleanor of Castile, the greatly loved wife of Edward I.

To the left of Whitehall is Northumberland Avenue running down to the River, on part of the ground occupied by the London house of the Dukes of Northumberland, which was pulled down in

1874, being the last of the long range of magnificent palaces belonging to the nobility which used to occupy the Southern side of the Strand, facing the River, which afforded a convenient route to the Palace of the Monarch, or to the Tower.

Seeing these things, you should begin to absorb the atmosphere of London—the fascinating mingling of yesterdays and to-day. London's dead past is alive.

We will now go down to the South Eastern corner of the Square, into the Strand. We will mount to the top of a bus, going East, to the Bank. Let others do what they will. Be ready to climb down now and then to pay a visit by the way.

Immediately, on the right hand, is Charing Cross railway station, opened in 1860, standing on the site of Hungerford Market, beside which was the blacking factory or warehouse in which Charles Dickens worked as a small, unhappy lad. His own account of his misery then is one of the most pathetic things in literature. This neighbourhood is somewhat thickly populated with memories of Dickens, as we shall soon see. Thus, nearly opposite the station is the Golden Cross Hotel, moved a bit Eastward from its original location, whence Mr. Samuel Pickwick and suite set out upon an immortal journey on top of the Rochester Coach. We can go there by motor coach to-day, and I advise you to do so. It is a pleasant jaunt, and you can eat and drink at the Bull at Rochester, with which hostelry if you are not acquainted, read the surprising adventures of the said Pickwick.

We could go down Villiers Street, on the East side of the station, turning to the left up Duke Street, and so into the charmingly old-world Adelphi.

So named after the brothers Adam, the architects of these streets and of many beautiful houses here and elsewhere, whose names were given to James, John and Robert Streets, William Street having been renamed Durham House Street, after the famous house that once stood here, wherein Sir Walter Raleigh dwelt for many years. This quarter is full of ghosts, many of whom it is pleasing to meet. On the Terrace, from which there is a glorious view of the river and the town, at No. 4 lived and died Robert and James Adam; Davy Garrick, actor and crotchety wit, at No. 5. Thomas Hardy lived for a while at No. 8. Round the corner in John Street is the Adelphi Hotel, where Mr. Pickwick and others were present and hilarious at a wedding feast. Close by is Buckingham Street, where young Mr. David Copperfield lodged. Samuel Pepys, he of that *Diary*, lived here in a house overlooking the River. At the foot of this street is one of the most interesting relics of old London life; the Water Gate of York House (PLATE II), built and designed by nobody exactly seems to know who, but probably by Nicholas Stone, "master mason of Whitehall and Windsor," in 1625. Very different then the life of London from what it is now. Then this gate stood on the edge of the River mud, and there my lords and ladies stepped down into their barges to go to Court or elsewhere a-visiting. York House, or York Place, was the town house of the Archbishops of York, but later came into lay hands, some of which were not too clean, including those of the Duke of Buckingham, in the reign of dull James II. But we must not linger too long.

To the old Londoner the Strand has lost much of

PLATE II

STATUE OF
KING CHARLES I

TRAFALGAR SQUARE

YORK HOUSE WATER GATE

PLATE III

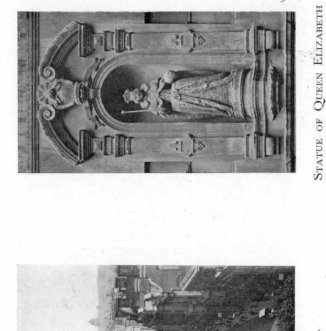

FLEET STREET
West of Temple Bar

STATUE OF QUEEN ELIZABETH
St. Dunstan's in the West

its charm and character, owing to rapid "improvements," which have made it much like any other prosperous thoroughfare in any other prosperous city. So we will bowl along, unheeding, except to note the pretty church of Saint Mary-le-Strand, of which Saint Thomas à Becket was rector and where John Dickens, father of Charles, was married on 13th June, 1809. North of it is the vast bulk of Bush House, an amazingly equipped and efficient block of "American" business offices, behind which is Kingsway, lined with office buildings, many of them occupied by well-known American firms.

The next church, also standing on an island, is Saint Clement Danes, built in 1681 by Sir Christopher Wren. There is a fine peal of bells in the tower, but they have nothing to do with "oranges and lemons." But the chief interest here is that you can sit in the pew, in the gallery, where Doctor Johnson worshipped and prayed.

Beyond the church, the huge Gothic pile on the left hand is the Royal Courts of Justice (PLATE III) looking like an overgrown religious house. Then in the middle of the road is a comic griffin, perched up, unworthily marking the site of Temple Bar, which was removed in 1878 as being a nuisance to the traffic. We are now in the City proper, as distinct from the town that has grown round it. In Fleet Street, as in the Strand, the hand of the improver has been at work, modernising the street out of all recognition. It used to be narrow, nice and nasty.

We will clamber down from our bus, or alight genteely from our car or taxi, to go into the Temple, entering it by the Gatehouse almost

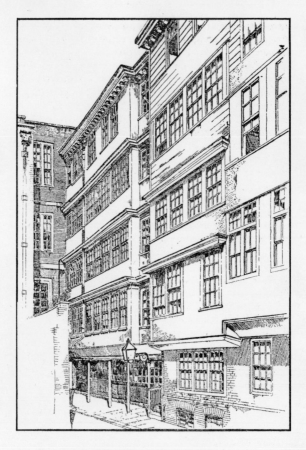

FIG. I. MIDDLE TEMPLE LANE

Drawn by Roland W. Paul, F.S.A.

18

opposite the Griffin and so into Middle Temple Lane (Fig. 1). This whole neighbourhood is, as a friend unkindly put it, "infested by lawyers." What is the Temple and why so-called I have often been asked when introducing American and other friends to it. Briefly, it is called the Temple because it used long ago to be the headquarters in England of the Knights Templars or "The Poor Knights of Christ and of the Temple of Solomon"; but they ceased to be poor, becoming proud and naughty, so they were suppressed and men of law eventually took their place. The Temple is known as an Inn of Law, of which there are four "majors," which alone have the right to "call" men and women to the Bar, hence Barristers, that is to authorise them to "practise." In a way they are much like the colleges at Oxford and Cambridge. In them barristers have "chambers," and solicitors and other legal folk have offices, and some few private persons are privileged to dwell here, and a very pleasant dwelling-place too. But at night somewhat ghostly.

The whole flavour of the Temple is delightfully old-world. The shades of famous men swarm in the courts and alleys. I know, for I have met many of them. I think that my chief ghost-friend is Doctor Oliver Goldsmith, who died at No. 2 Brick Court, Middle Temple Lane, where he and his friends used to make night merry. Charles Lamb was born at No. 2 Crown Office Row, overlooking the gardens where, in Henry VI, the men of York and Lancaster plucked the red and white roses. But the gardens and the roses were different from those of to-day, the flowers being similar to the white and red roses that adorn the hedges of our

19

country roads and fields. Lamb lived in the Temple with his sister Mary, first in No. 16 Mitre Court Buildings and later at No. 4 Inner Temple Lane. But the ruthless improvers have destroyed both houses. Thackeray had chambers at No. 10 Crown Office Row; and in Lamb Building, hard by the church, Arthur Pendennis and George Warrington read, wrote, smoked and drank, and were visited by the amiable and astonished Major Pendennis; and pretty Fanny Bolton looked up longingly at the windows in the dusk of the evening. When going down Middle Temple Lane, you must turn aside to visit Fountain Court (PLATE V), where John Westcott wooed and won Ruth Pinch. Then go into Middle Temple Hall (PLATE IV), a beautiful room, with a grand open timber roof (Fig. 2), built in the days of Queen Elizabeth.

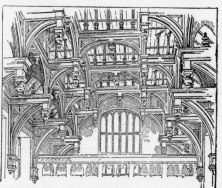

FIG. 2. THE ROOF, MIDDLE TEMPLE HALL
Drawn by Sir Banister Fletcher, P.R.I.B.A.

20

Here, almost for certain, William Shakespeare, gentleman, poet, playwright, actor and theatrical manager, took part in a performance of "Twelfth Night" upon the second of February, 1601-2. It is good to linger here awhile, peering into the dim but brilliant past; thinking of some of those who have supped here : Queen Bess herself, maybe; Sir Walter Raleigh ; Congreve and Wycherley ; Henry Fielding, possibly entertaining Mr. Tom Jones; Tommy Moore; de Quincey ; Dickens — many more. If you are an American, and should chance to be here upon the fourth of July, remember that of the signers of the Declaration of Independence, Rutledge, Heywood, McKean, Lynch and Middleton were members of the Inner Temple.

We must not forget to go into the church of Saint Mary, commonly called the Temple Church,

Fig. 3. St. Martin Ludgate

Drawn by Sir Andrew T. Taylor, F.S.A.

one of the four round churches in England. If the door is shut, knock and you will probably be admitted. The round portion of the building dates as far back as 1185, being circular after the style of the Church of the Holy Sepulchre

21

in Jerusalem. The choir was added in 1240. Despite the deeds of the restorer the place is deeply impressive.

Out of the sombre shadows. Turn round to the right, look at a lowly grave in the shadow of the trees, and stand reverent, for " Here lies Oliver Goldsmith" (PLATE IV). Then up the narrow way back to Fleet Street, crossing it, and walking Eastward a short distance, until we reach the narrow entry of Wine Office Court, where is the old Cheshire Cheese tavern, an ancient house of entertainment, where we can lunch or dine or sup with great satisfaction, and sit in the chair where maybe Doctor Johnson sat, or perhaps did not, for we have no knowledge that the Doctor frequented this tavern, but probably he did do so. Charles Dickens certainly did come here to enjoy the "red hot chop" of which he was fond or to partake of the famous pudding. There used to be a parrot here who swore beautifully; but, alas, he has gone the way of all men and birds. If you do dine here, do not forget to drink

FIG. 4. BELL TOWER, ST. PAUL'S CATHEDRAL

Drawn by Sir Andrew T. Taylor, F.S.A.

PLATE IV

OLIVER GOLDSMITH'S TOMB
In the Temple Churchyard

MIDDLE TEMPLE HALL

PLATE V

THE GREAT HALL, CHARTERHOUSE

FOUNTAIN COURT, THE TEMPLE

one or more glasses of fine Port wine in the very
enticing cellars.

We will walk across Ludgate Circus and up Ludgate Hill (note St. Martin Ludgate Fig. 3), which
leads steeply to Saint Paul's (Fig. 4). We have left
the land of law and newspapers and St. Bride's
(Fig. 5), and are now in a religious quarter. The
names of the streets and
lanes hereabout carry us
back to old Saint Paul's:
Paternoster Row, Amen
Corner, Ave Maria Lane.
Stand a while at the foot
of Ludgate Hill, looking
to Saint Paul's, the dome
(*Frontispiece*, PLATE 1),
perhaps seeming almost
snow white against a
background of smoky,
sombre cloud; sometimes
dreamy grey against a
blue sky; sometimes al-
most invisible, wrapped
in wisps of drifting rain or
yellow fog; always with
the slender, black flèche
of St. Martin's piercing
upwards curiously con-
trasting with the great
mass beyond. Wren built
this great dome to domi-
nate a small London; it is
still the centre of a
London vaster than can
ever have entered his

FIG. 5. ST. BRIDE'S,
FLEET STREET

*Drawn by Sir Andrew
T. Taylor, F.S.A.*

23

dreams; whether seen from the hills of Kent across the river, or the heights of Highgate and Hampstead. It is seldom remembered that this is the first Protestant cathedral built in England; queerly enough James II hoped it would be Roman Catholic. The interior is even more solemnly impressive than the exterior, with a more masculine beauty than that of Westminster Abbey.

We will now mount our bus again, for a short time, passing through Saint Paul's Churchyard, which is a centre of the wholesale drapery trade. Immediately on the right is the way into Doctors' Commons, where both David Copperfield and Charles Dickens worked.

Then through Queen Victoria Street to the Mansion House, the official home of the Lord Mayor of London. The space before it is probably the busiest scene of traffic in the world. At least it is so on week-days, but at night-time, on Saturday afternoons and all Sunday, it is almost desolate. A saunter about the City streets late on a moonlight night is a weird experience. It is scarcely worth while going into the Mansion House, which is vast, gloomy, almost dreary, and not even ancient, dating from about the middle of the eighteenth century. Across the way are the Bank of England, where the money comes from and goes to, and the Royal Exchange, no more the supreme centre of the business transactions of the country, as it was in the days of its first predecessor, built by merchant prince Sir Thomas Gresham in 1570 and burned in the Great Fire of 1666. Inside are some modern wall-pictures, illustrating the story of English commerce and so forth, which some people admire and some do not.

This part of the City has never greatly appealed to me; somehow it is not very Londony; so I am always glad to turn West, into the Poultry and Cheapside, where old London comes back to me. The Poultry is so-called because here long since were many poulterers' shops; Cheapside because it ran along the side of the ancient chepe or open market-place of the City, as is still betokened by such names as Bread Street, where John Milton was born, Milk Street, where genial Sir Thomas More was born, and so on. There is a very literary flavour about Cheapside and some of the near-by streets. There is Bird-in-Hand Court, where Keats lived for a time and wrote his first volume of poems. There is Bow Church, with the lovely steeple; Saint Mary-le-Bow (Fig. 6); Bow Bells, the hearing of which when you enter into the world makes you a true born "Cockney." But much depends upon the direction from which the

FIG. 6. ST. MARY-LE-BOW, CHEAPSIDE

Drawn by Sir Andrew T. Taylor, F.S.A.

E   25

wind is blowing. It was these bells that called back
Dick Whittington to be three times Mayor of
London. But not from Highgate!

Go down Bow Lane for the jolly little Georgian
court, and its iron screen.

Somewhere between Bread Street and Friday
Street stood the Mermaid Tavern, where Shakespeare, Ben Jonson, Raleigh, Donne, Beaumont
and Fletcher and many other worthies fore-
gathered, imbibing a vast deal of sack and Rhenish,
with probably very small accompaniment of bread.
If you like to go down Bread Street where Milton
was baptized in the vanished Church of Allhallows,
you will find St. Mildred's, with its fine plaster-
vaulted Wren interior.

Behind the small shop at the corner of Wood
Street, pursuing our Westward way, is the famous
plane-tree, of which Wordsworth wrote:

> "At the corner of Wood Street, when daylight appears,
> Hangs a thrush that sings loud, it has sung for three years:
> Poor Susan has pass'd by the spot, and has heard
> In the silence of morning the song of the bird."

But he omits to mention the tree!

Go up Wood Street, turn along Silver Street to the
corner of Monkwell Street: where Shakespeare
lodged in 1604 with Christopher Montjoy, in the
love affair of whose daughter he played a part.

We are now on the North side of St Paul's Churchyard, where the fine Chapter-house is to-day partly
a bank. There are many lanes round booky
Paternoster Row, and in Panyers Alley is the
"naked boy" tablet (Fig. 7) which marks, errone-
ously some say, the City's highest point. In Foster
Lane is the church of St. Vedast Foster, one of
Wren's happiest interiors and most graceful spires.

We now go along Newgate Street, in which there is not much of interest, since Christ's Hospital, better known as the Blue Coat School, departed to

FIG. 7. SCULPTURED STONE IN
PANYERS ALLEY

Drawn by John Wykeham Archer

the country; Charles Lamb, Coleridge and Leigh Hunt were schoolboys there, and Elia (pronounced Ellia) immortalised it in his Essay on

27

"Christ's Hospital Five-and-Thirty Years Ago." Lamb loved and understood London more fully than any other writer, not excepting Charles Dickens.

On reaching the end of Newgate Street, note, as the guide-books say, the handsome church of Saint Sepulchre, which goes back to the days of the Crusades, but which has been badly mauled by nineteenth century "restorers" and was not kindly treated by the Great Fire. Until the year 1890 the bells here were tolled when a man or a woman was hung at grim Newgate, just round the corner, and previously to 1774 when a poor wight set forth on his journey to Tyburn Tree. Captain John Smith of Virginia sleeps here.

We may now leave the direct route, turning up Giltspur Street to Smithfield, originally perhaps "smooth field," where tournaments used to be held, where there was a famous horse and cattle market, where there were executions, where Wat Tyler was slain by Sir William Walworth, Mayor of London, and where in the reigns of Mary and Elizabeth, men and women went to a fiery death for their faiths. Here, from 1133 to 1840 was held Bartholomew Fair, which became such a scene of rioting and scandalous conduct that it was suppressed. In the East corner is one of the oldest churches in London, Saint Bartholomew the Great, or, rather, a small remaining portion of what must have been a very splendid building, a wonderful example of Norman architecture. Go in. Near the church is Bartholomew Close, where John Milton sought refuge when Charles II came to his own; where Hogarth was born, and where Benjamin Franklin lodged, when he was working as a printer in the Lady Chapel of Saint Bartholomew's, when it was used as a printery!

We go on to Charterhouse Square, where men and women of fashion used to reside, but which interests us because William Makepeace Thackeray lodged there when a lad attending Charterhouse School. It is a curious testimony to the living appeal of great characters in fiction that they haunt the places where we are told they lived almost as vividly as do those who really dwelt there. It is so with the Charterhouse (PLATE V), which was first a Carthusian priory, whose last Prior was executed by Henry VIII because he desired to continue in the faith in which he had been brought up. We cannot follow all the vicissitudes of the Charterhouse, but will note that it was purchased in 1611 by Thomas Sutton, an Elizabethan adventurer and subject of James I, who endowed it as the "hospital of King James," for eighty poor brethren or pensioners, "gentlemen by descent and in poverty," and for the maintenance and education of forty boys. The pensioners were to be sixty in number. In 1872 the school was removed to Godalming in Surrey. But I, and you, too, I trust, go to the Charterhouse not only to see the charming buildings, or because Richard Lovelace, Roger Williams, the founder of Rhode Island, Dicky Steele, Joseph Addison, John Wesley, John Leech and Thackeray were boys there, but mainly to see the old Hall in which Colonel Newcome dined and the old Chapel in which he worshipped. The Charterhouse is one of the most notable and most restfully beautiful places in London. There is no other spot where one can more fully forget to-day and go back to yesterday.

29

We now return to Holborn and progress on our Westward way.

Beside Saint Sepulchre's, running down to the right, is Snow Hill, which has two curiously different literary connections. Here John Bunyan died in 1688, and here was the Saracen's Head Inn, whence Mr. Squeers and Mr. Nicholas Nickleby set out on the coach for Yorkshire. At the bottom of the Hill, turning to the left we can go up the stone steps on to Holborn Viaduct, which crosses the street that covers the Fleet river. Proceeding Westward, on the left is the church of Saint Andrew (Fig. 8), where in 1808 William Hazlitt was married, Charles Lamb being best man and Mary Lamb a bridesmaid. Here in 1817 Benjamin Disraeli was received into the church of England, an event that made his career as a politician possible.

FIG. 8. ST. ANDREW'S, HOLBORN

Drawn by Sir Andrew T. Taylor, F.S.A.

The big "junction" at Holborn Circus gives access to a few interesting spots. Thavies Inn is a curious little corner; the Bartlett's Buildings door-

ways are jolly, while a little farther on the old
Hall of Barnard's Inn is used as a school. North
of the Circus Hatton Garden, the diamond centre,
is St. Andrew's delightful old school. In the
quiet backwater of Ely Place, where the beadle
shuts the gates every night, is the early fourteenth
century church of St. Etheldreda, once the
chapel of the palace of the Bishop of Ely. Wise
folk go to see it.

For a time there is nothing exciting to see, until
on the left we reach a picturesque group of Elizabethan houses, gabled and timbered (PLATE VI),
called Staple Inn. The Hall of 1581, with open
timber roof, lies at the back of a pleasant paved
court, with ornamental gardens beyond. A quiet
restful, shadowy place it is. Imagine the streets of
London lined with such houses, with here a
church and there the statelier home of a nobleman
or rich merchant, and you will be looking at the
London of Shakespeare. He must often have seen
these very houses when visiting his friend and
patron Lord Southampton in his home at the
corner of Chancery Lane and Holborn. We will
go down the Lane until we reach on the right the
fine brick gateway of Lincoln's Inn, built in
1518. It is worth strolling in to see the old-world
buildings (Fig. 9) and the refreshing greenery.
Into Lincoln's Inn Fields (PLATE VI), beyond,
turning sharp to the right, and so by the Great
Turnstile back into Holborn. Cross, and a little
to the East, is the entrance to the fourth of the
great Inns of Court, Gray's Inn, which was a
dwelling-place of men of law as long since as the
fourteenth century. It is a quiet, pleasant place to
wander in. There is the old dining Hall to see,

31

FIG. 9. OLD SQUARE, LINCOLN'S INN

Drawn by Roland W. Paul, F.S.A.

32

where in 1594 "The Comedy of Errors" was played at the Christmas revels. The delightful garden may have been laid out by Francis Bacon, who is said to have planted a tree therein, which still more or less flourishes. Gray's Inn is redolent of Elizabethan days: among the members having been Nicholas, father of Francis Bacon; Sir Thomas Gresham and Lord Burleigh. On grand days in the Hall a toast is drunk to "the glorious, pious and immortal memory of Queen Elizabeth." Nathaniel Hawthorne wrote truly that it is like magic to "find yourself transported from the jumble, mob, tumult, uproar . . . into what seems an eternal Sabbath."

We must hasten or we shall never get home to-day. We can do so now for there is nothing much to be done in the way of exploration along New Oxford Street and Oxford Street, unless you insist on turning aside, Northward, up Museum Street to visit the British Museum. I will not escort you, holding a museum to be a dreary record of dead pasts. I prefer to mingle with the living, dead or alive; let the dead hob-nob with the dead.

As we journey Westward, the change is notable that takes place in the social atmosphere. The folk are more smartly dressed and in less of a hurry. Great shops and stores take the place of blocks of office buildings, and there are many promises of merriment by night: theatres, cinemas, restaurants, cafés.

So we go on until we reach the North-East corner of Hyde Park, the Marble Arch; Park Lane running almost due South, and Edgware Road almost due North. Close to the opening of the last a stone let into the roadway marks the site of Tyburn

Tree, where many malefactors expiated their sins and many saints suffered for virtues. The horrid scenes here enacted ceased in 1759. Among those whose lives were suspended here were Claude Duval, Jack Sheppard, Jonathan Wild, Perkin Warbeck, Lord Ferrers, one of the few of our ancient nobility who rose to eminence as a criminal, and—if you desire to know more I must refer you elsewhere for the sorry record. In past days Oxford Street was called the Tyburn Road; the road from ruin to death.

Let us leave these cheerless memories, turning down Park Lane, once the abode of nobility, gentry and rich somebodies, but the stately homes of London have given place to huge hotels, apartment houses and—oh, horror!—places of business. But not all the glory has departed, for there remains and cannot be taken away the beauty of Hyde Park.

Across the West end of Piccadilly and down Constitution Hill to Buckingham Palace, along on the right being the charming gardens pertaining thereto. The palace is more big than beautiful. Here was the mulberry garden planted by ineffable James I, that worm of a man who desired to breed silkworms. Inside, of course, the palace is sumptuous and contains a notable collection of pictures; but as we may not go in, why worry about them? Then we will stroll along the Mall, the Northern boundary of pretty Saint James's Park, where naughty Charles II played at "pail-mail" with his courtiers, flirted with the reigning mistress and fed the birds. After Queen Elizabeth, I should like to meet the gay Charles more than any other monarch. He is worthy of more respect than many respect-

34

able men. About half-way along the Mall is Saint James's Palace, the building of which was commenced by beastly Henry VIII. Here the Court was moved when Whitehall was burned in 1698, and here it still technically remains, ambassadors being accredited to the Court of Saint James. It is an abode of many sad ghosts. Here died Queen Mary of tragic memory; here Charles I parted from his children before he set out to walk across the Park in the falling snow to the scaffold at Whitehall. But it is in a homely way a picturesque pile and contains several fine rooms. The changing of the guard in the Friary Court, between 10.30 and 11 a.m., is a stately ceremony worth seeing if you have time and inclination. The drumming and the trumpeting are quite stirring! On the East side of the narrow way leading from the Park to Pall Mall is Marlborough House, where for many years lived the "Prince," afterward Edward VII, and the "Princess," afterward Queen Alexandra, the well-beloved. It is not an exciting place to look at, but within it is interesting. It was built in 1710 by Sir Christopher Wren for the Great Duke of Marlborough. King George was born there in 1865. So from Henry VIII and in truth much earlier, down to these present days, roundabout Saint James's has been enacted much of the Court history of England.

We pass on along the Mall, under the Admiralty arch and into Trafalgar Square.

We have been many miles together, round the town, seeing something of its present and more of its past. If you have enjoyed yourself I am rewarded. Of course you are not bound to follow the Tour exactly as laid out; you can part with me where you will, spending your time chiefly upon what you most enjoy. If you wish to do the route thoroughly, it will take you far more than the inside of one day.

PLATE VI

STAPLE INN, HOLBORN

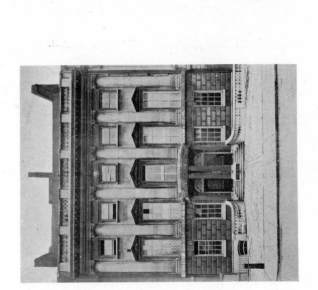

57 AND 58 LINCOLN'S INN FIELDS

PLATE VII

THE BANQUETING HOUSE, WHITEHALL

WESTMINSTER ABBEY
Showing Henry VII's Chapel and the Chapter House

SECOND TOUR

ROUTE: Trafalgar Square; Whitehall; Parliament Street; Houses of Parliament; Westminster Abbey; Westminster School; Victoria Embankment; Blackfriars; Queen Victoria Street; Cannon Street; London Bridge; The Monument; Eastcheap; Great Tower Street; The Tower.

SETTING out again from Trafalgar Square, we will go Southward, past the statue of Charles I, and so into Whitehall, so called after the great palace built there by Cardinal Wolsey, who discreetly handed it over to his master, Henry VIII. The right side of the street is almost entirely occupied by Government offices which are not even worth looking at! The left hand is far more interesting. Of the famous home of the Tudors and Stuarts all that remains is the Banqueting Hall (PLATE VII), built in the reign of James I, the architect being Inigo Jones. Through one of the windows, but exactly which one nobody knows, Charles I went out on to the scaffold in the year 1649, and herein William of Orange and Mary his wife accepted the Crown in 1689 from the Lords and Commons. The building is now occupied by the Royal United Service Museum.

On the opposite side of the road is Downing Street, where since 1735 Prime Ministers have come and gone. Queer stories its walls could tell, making some and marring other reputations.

The continuation of Whitehall is known as Parliament Street. In the centre of the way is the Cenotaph, erected to the memory of British citizens who died in the Great War. It has a dignified simplicity too often lacking in British memorials. Here each year is celebrated with solemn splendour the anniversary of Armistice day.

On the left Derby Street leads to New Scotland Yard, the appropriately sombre home of the Metropolitan Police.

We are now in Westminster, though the actual boundaries of that City extend very far and wide, roughly from Temple Bar in the East to Chelsea in the West, from the Thames up to Oxford Street. But it is about what is popularly known as Westminster that we will now roam.

The big open space is Parliament Square, as stupidly misused in the way of statuary as are most of the open places of London. The statues are dreadful with the exception of the replica of that of Abraham Lincoln by Saint Gaudens, close by the Middlesex Town Hall, which is not so bad a building for these days. Near to it is one of London's unholiest horrors, a drinking-fountain designed by Sir Gilbert Scott, of whom it can be said that "he never touched anything that he did adorn."

The Houses of Parliament, a mass of sham Gothic, appeal to the true lover of London only because of Westminster Hall, which is both ancient and lovely. There can be few more impressive interiors, few more attractive to those who like to wander into the past. It must be ghostly in the dark hours

FIG. 10. WESTMINSTER ABBEY FROM DEAN'S YARD

Drawn by Herbert Railton

39

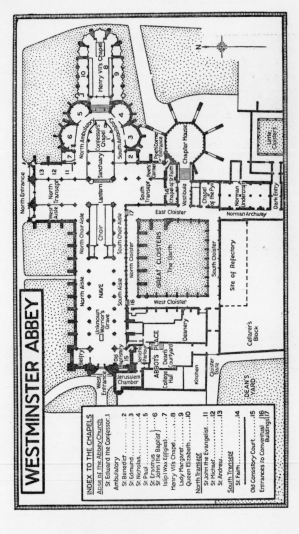

WESTMINSTER ABBEY

INDEX TO THE CHAPELS

Apse of the Abbey Church

St Edward the Confessor...1

Ambulatory

St Benedict...2
St Edmund...3
St Nicholas...4
St Paul...5
St Erasmus...6
St John the Baptist}...7
Islip (Wax Effigies)...8
Henry VII's Chapel...9
Queen Elizabeth...10

North Transept

St John the Evangelist...11
St Michael...12
St Andrew...13

South Transept

St Faith...14

Old Consistory Court...15
Entrances to Conventual [16
Buildings]17

Fig. II. Plan of Westminster Abbey

before the dawn. Here Edward II was kicked off his unsteady throne, and Richard II, who was greatly responsible for its erection, kicked himself off his. There have been famous and fatal trials here: William Wallace; Sir Thomas More; Elizabeth's Lord Essex; Guy Fawkes; Lord Strafford and his weak friend Charles I; Warren Hastings. Here King Edward VII lay in state. The roof, of sturdy Sussex oak, is a skilful and beautiful example of a Master Carpenter's work. Look up; look around; and dream.

We will now walk across the Square, to the North door of Westminster Abbey (Fig. 11), and enter. What shall I say? The less the better. I first knew the Abbey when a schoolboy, having the privilege of roaming all over it, free and unattended. My advice is this; if you cannot spend many hours here, be content with gaining a general impression of its almost overwhelming beauty. Next to the appeal made by the grace and loveliness of the building, comes the fascination of the ancient monuments. English history springs to life here and in the Tower.

Poet's Corner? Does that greatly interest you? I would rather go where great writers have lived and worked than where they rest. The Abbey belongs to Kings and Queens, Princes and Princesses and great nobles. In the sanctuary sleeps Anne of Cleves, fourth victim of Henry Bluebeard; and is not the very name of Aymer de Valence a note of music? The shrine of Saint Edward the Confessor, mutilated though it be, summons a vision of dead superstitions, of the days when pilgrims, of high and low degree, sincere and insincere, came from near and far, by land and by sea, to pray and make offering at the shrines of saints, asking for health of body in this world and for salvation of soul in the world to come. Here and at Canterbury all this lives again. It was right that Dan Chaucer should be buried here.

Of the monarchs that lie here we will certainly look at the tombs of Edward I and his Queen, Eleanor of Castile; Henry V and Queen Kate; Henry VII, in his gorgeous chapel; Queen Mary; Queen Elizabeth; and Mary, Queen of Scots. And Henry VII's Chapel (PLATE VII), with amazing, too ornate roof.

In the South aisle of the nave are two small doors, used of yore by the monks, through either of which we can go into the Cloisters (Fig. 12). Here we come into close touch with the conventual life with which they and the surrounding buildings were once so busy. Walk round, drinking in the old-world atmosphere. Perhaps glancing at some of the tombs and monuments: the great actor Betterton lies here, his successor Henry Irving being in the Abbey; on the wall a tablet with the appealing words, "Jane Lister, dear Childe." From the South walk, on a day of mixed sunshine and shadow, there is a lovely view of the Abbey; behind us is the monks' Refectory. From the East walk a passage leads to the Chapter House, a beautifully graceful chamber, where from the time of Edward III until the middle of the sixteenth century the House of Commons sat and talked, as before them the rulers of the Abbey sat and talked. But now the Dean and Chapter sit and talk in the Jerusalem Chamber, which we will visit by and by.

Returning to the Cloisters, turn to the left, and to

FIG. 12. THE CLOISTERS, WESTMINSTER ABBEY

Drawn by E. Tarver

the left again, along a dark low passage into the
Little Cloisters, a pretty, peaceful corner, occupying the site of the monks' Infirmary, where now
dwell fortunate ecclesiastics and musicians. The
coolth here is welcome on a hot day, but it is
rather draughty and chilling in winter-time.
Back again, and turning left, we are quickly in
Little Dean's Yard, which is for the most part
surrounded by buildings belonging to Westminster
School (PLATE VIII). The visitor from overseas
may not have time to see Eton, Harrow or Win-
chester; but an hour at Westminster will put him
in touch with the life and atmosphere of all our
great public schools. "Westminster," the College
of Saint Peter at Westminster, is the offspring of the
Abbey, nestling like an aged chick under the guardian wing of its still more aged mother. Trustworthy tradition carries its beginnings back to ancient days, but for practical purposes it is a founda-
tion of Queen Elizabeth, who dissolved the monastic
establishment brought to new life by Queen Mary.
In term time a Saturday afternoon, or any day out
of term, we are allowed to saunter round the
buildings. On our left, as we enter the Yard from
the Cloisters, is a stone gateway, from which a
flight of stone steps leads up to "school." The
big schoolroom was the dorter or dormitory of the
monks and is still somewhat austere. Also, somewhat spoiled by the rather churchy rows of chairs,
the modern panelling and the electric chandeliers.
Our guide, probably the school sergeant, will tell
many things of interest about the doings in "school"
will show you the old oak table, in the drawer of
which birches are kept for the just chastisement of
naughty boys; and, close by, the form upon which

PLATE VIII

St. Helen's Bishopsgate

The Gateway, Westminster
School

PLATE IX

VICTORIA EMBANKMENT AND THE HOUSES OF PARLIAMENT

VICTORIA EMBANKMENT AND WATERLOO BRIDGE

"J. Dryden" cut his name. This brings us up against the tradition that stands behind every old public school, which is an inspiration to the boys of to-day not merely to cut their names upon wood or stone but to write them on the pages of English history. Others who were boys here were Richard Hakluyt; Ben Jonson; George Herbert; Abraham Cowley; Sir Christopher Wren; John Locke; Mat Prior; Samuel and Charles Wesley; William Cowper; Warren Hastings; Edward Gibbon; Jeremy Bentham; Robert Southey; Lord John Russell; James Anthony Froude.

As we go "down school" we shall be shown the Busby Library, built by that famous headmaster; a charming room, with a fine modelled plaster ceiling in high relief containing many of his books. Then down the steps into the Yard, and to Ashburnham House, where is the school library and other matters; the staircase, probably by John Webb, about 1640, is a masterpiece of Renaissance art. Then under an old archway into Dean's Yard, with its fine trees and beautiful view of the Abbey. To the right, again to the right, and to the left into a quiet courtyard, up quaint wooden steps into College Hall, formerly the Abbot's dining-room and now that of the King's Scholars: with a fine timbered roof, minstrels' gallery, and heavy tables, reputed to be made of the wood of ships of the wonderful, woeful Armada. In the far corner is an entrance to the Jerusalem Chamber, which was the Abbot's retiring-room.

Passing through the Abbey, and out by the door whereby we came in, we should spend a few minutes in Saint Margaret's church, which would receive more attention were it not dominated by the Abbey. Though it bears the mark of the restorer, it is still beautiful. Many famous folk are buried in the church and churchyard: William Caxton, whose printery was close by; Sir Walter Raleigh, who was executed not far away, are among them. Most of the glass is modern, but not ugly or uninteresting. There are windows to the memory of Milton, given by G. W. Childs of Philadelphia; to Raleigh, also from American goodwill; and a fine East window, said to celebrate the espousal of Catherine of Arragon and Prince Arthur, but which may do nothing of the kind; those anti-quarians do differ; it is their life-blood. This window was buried to escape the zeal of the Puritans, who are discredited with many more artistic crimes than they committed. Was it not a Puritan who wrote:

> "But let my due feet never fail
> To walk the studious cloister's pale,
> And love the high embowe'd roof,
> With antique pillars massy proof,
> And storied windows richly dight
> Casting a dim religious light:
> There let the pealing organ blow
> To the full-voiced quire below,
> As may with sweetness, through mine ear,
> Dissolve me into ecstacies. . ."

Now we must back to the garishness of modernity, crossing Parliament Square, glancing up at Big Ben (PLATE IX), as the clock on the tower of the Houses is called, and refusing to believe that the minute hand is fourteen feet long. Time is short. We must pause on Westminster Bridge to see the view, of which I will not be so foolish as to attempt a description, but will quote the sonnet

46

by Wordsworth "Composed upon Westminster Bridge" in September 1802:

> "Earth has not anything to show more fair:
> Dull would he be of soul who could pass by
> A sight so touching in its majesty:
> This City now doth like a garment wear
> The beauty of the morning: silent, bare,
> Ships, towers, domes, theatres, and temples lie
> Open unto the fields, and to the sky,
> All bright and glittering in the smokeless air.
> Never did sun more beautifully steep
> In his first splendour valley, rock, or hill;
> Ne'er saw I, never felt, a calm so deep!
> The river glideth at his own sweet will:
> Dear God! the very houses seem asleep;
> And all that mighty heart is lying still."

Though the scene has greatly changed, the majesty remains; he did see the tower of Lambeth Palace, home for centuries of the Archbishops of Canterbury; he did not see the Houses of Parliament, or New Scotland Yard, or—on the right as we look down stream—the London County Hall. He saw a muddy, squalid foreshore on both banks; not the fine Victoria Embankment (PLATE IX) on the left. We will take a "car" along it to Blackfriars, sitting on top so that we may enjoy the view to the full. Hideous Charing Cross Railway bridge has one attraction, that it marks the site of Hungerford Market, a centre of Dickens memories. Immediately after passing under it, look on the left over the gardens, and you see Adelphi Terrace. Then the huge piles of offices and of Savoy Hotels. Then Waterloo Bridge, and on the left the stately façade of Somerset House. And so to Blackfriars Bridge, whose name commemorates the monastery that once occupied the ground where now are *The Times* office and the lower end of Queen Victoria Street, along which we may as well walk. There is little to note in it, except just beyond *The Times* the church of Saint Andrew by the Wardrobe, so called because hereabouts used to be a building in which the Masters of the Wardrobe kept His Majesty's apparel of state and which was removed after the Great Fire. *Don't* miss Wren's lovely little brick church of St. Benet's, Paul's Wharf, just below the street opposite. Go to service if you want an experience, the Anglican liturgy being rendered in Welsh!

A bit farther on, on the North, standing back from the street, is the home of the College of Arms, where coats of arms are granted and pedigrees traced back to Adam.

Farther on we will turn to the right into Cannon Street, of which the name is a good example of the historic interest that attaches to so many London street names. It was once Candlewick or Candlewright Street. John Stow says that it "took that name (as may be supposed) either of chandlers, or makers of candles, both of wax and tallow; for candlewright is a maker of candles, or of wick which is the cotton or yarn thereof, or otherwise wike," wike being a "working place." It was one of the earliest City thoroughfares. Act IV, scene 6, of "The Second Part of King Henry VI" is laid in Cannon Street, so say modern editions of the play, but it should of course be Candlewick street, when Jack Cade sat upon London stone. This feat you cannot perform, the stone now being encaged in the wall of Saint Swithin's church, opposite Cannon Street railway station. Where this stone came from and what it signifies nobody knows, though lots of people say they do. Saint Swithin's Lane leads to the Mansion House, but we are not that way bent, nor are we turning right along Queen Street over Southwark Bridge, but let's have a look at those glorious twin doorways of 1704 on Laurence Pountney Hill. We are going along Cannon Street, until we see the statue of King William IV, where this street, King William Street, Gracechurch Street and Eastcheap converge. Just about where this not too lovely statue stands was once the Boar's Head tavern, where Sir John Falstaff and his friends made merry. At least, they would have done so had the tavern existed in their day. But we may feel sure that Shakespeare and his companions did drink sack and Rhenish there, and that he saw Sir John and Prince Hal in his mind's eye, possibly finding a model there for the former. Doctor Oliver Goldsmith cracked a bottle there: sitting "by a pleasant fire, in the very room where old Sir John Falstaff cracked his jokes, in the very chair which was sometimes honoured by Prince Henry, and sometimes polluted by his immoral merry companions." Alack, that we cannot obtain any refreshment there.

Southward is London Bridge (PLATE X). Let us go down to it, and standing against the parapet, look down stream into the Pool of London, at the busy ships. The view upstream, too, is interesting. Crossing the bridge, we are in Southwark, on Bankside, filled with memories of Shakespeare. There in the Church of Saint Saviour his younger brother Edmund was buried in 1607. There, also, lie Philip Massinger; John G. Gower, poet friend of Chaucer; William Emerson, possibly an ancestor of "our American friend"; and many other worthies. To Americans the Harvard Chapel is particularly interesting. John Harvard, founder of Harvard, was born in Southwark in 1607, and baptised in this church. Among the many "literary" windows here, are those dedicated to Doctor Goldsmith and Doctor Johnson, both of whom knew this neighbourhood well; Bunyan; Chaucer; Beaumont and Fletcher; Massinger; and Shakespeare. You may linger here, if you will, but we should be getting along. If you keep your eyes open, you may meet the shades of Jack Cade in the street; of Chaucer's Canterbury Pilgrims, who set out from the Tabard Inn in Borough High Street; Mr. Pickwick and Samuel Weller, who met in the George Inn; and others. Behind the prosaic goods yard door lies the galleried fragment of the George Inn; let us rejoice over it and patronise its old tap room. Not far away are remnants of the Marshalsea Prison, of which Little Dorrit was the child, and in Saint George's church she was baptised, but you will not find her name in the register. Lant Street, too, where Dickens lodged as a small boy, his father being resident in the Marshalsea, and he himself working at the blacking factory, at Hungerford Bridge as aforesaid. The riotous and jolly Bob Sawyer had "diggings" here. He was, of course, a student at Guy's Hospital, which is tucked away beyond the big station, and in spite of modern developments keeps some of its original eighteenth century character.

Back across London Bridge, into Fish Street Hill, where is the Monument, memorial of the Great Fire, which began close by in Pudding Lane on September the second, 1666. This is not the only

PLATE X

LONDON BRIDGE

PLATE XI

THE TOWER OF LONDON AND THE TOWER BRIDGE

monument that lies! There's a glorious view over London from the top cage, if you don't mind struggling up some hundreds of worn steps.

If you wish to see a queer by-street of London and do not mind the smell of fish, ask your way to Lower Thames Street and go East along it. Close to London Bridge is the church of Saint Magnus the Martyr, with a beautiful Wren steeple. Then we reach Billingsgate Market, headquarters of the London fish trade; where the porters used to use very shocking language, whence "Billingsgate!" Farther along, on the same side, is the Custom House. Then soon we are on Tower Hill; and there is the Tower of London (PLATE XI). What impression is made on grown-ups when first they see the Tower, of which they have heard, or, perhaps read so much? Like many another Londoner I saw it first when a small boy, and was curious rather than interested. Now it takes me back to the black deeds and horrors of mediæval and Tudor England. They were bitter cruel then; human life was held lightly by those who took it and awful tortures of mind and body were inflicted upon the living. The Tower is a whited sepulchre whose stones are red with blood. As at Westminster Abbey, one wishes it was permitted to wander here alone. But the greatly privileged only are allowed to do so, and then not quite alone, for a guide must be with them.

The Tower has often been described as a fortress, a palace and a prison, but it is as the last that I am driven to think of it. The tale of terror is almost endless, and pitiable. There have been many murders here, judicial and other: Henry VI; the Duke of Clarence and his brother—the "Princes in the Tower," regarding whose fate there is still mystery; Protector Somerset, who could not protect his own head; the Duke of Buckingham, victim of Henry VIII, who made such a fine speech according to Shakespeare; sad Lady Jane Grey; and Elizabeth's Earl of Essex. During the War spies met their death here. Of prisoners who escaped the scaffold, a veritable multitude: James I, poet King of Scotland; Elizabeth, who was afterward here as Queen. These two seem to be the most live ghosts. Here Henry VIII married Catherine of Arragon and Anne Boleyn. Here Charles II spent the night before his Coronation, being the last King of England to sleep in the Tower. But as we go round with our guide, there is a sense almost of unreality about the places we are shown and the stories we are told. There is too much of the museum atmosphere.

The great White Tower, the oldest part of the fortress, begun by William the Conqueror, is very museumy. But nothing can allay the wonder of the Norman Chapel of Saint John (Figs. 13 and 14), perhaps the oldest church of Christ in London City. There are the Bell Tower; Saint Thomas's Tower, over the Traitors' Gate; Beauchamp Tower; the Bloody Tower; and so on. Each with a story of woe. Tower Green, with the ominous ravens, where Anne Boleyn, Catherine Howard, Lady Jane Grey, the Earl of Essex, were done to death. Hard by is the church of Saint Peter ad Vincula, where those just named and others were buried. A note of gay colour is struck by the uniform of the Yeomen Warders, which dates from early Tudor days; they are popularly known as Beefeaters, perhaps because they were eaters of beef.

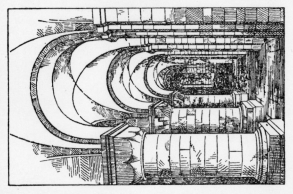

St. John's Chapel, Tower of London

Fig. 13. South Aisle

Fig. 14. View looking East

Let us escape from this prison house, going along Tower Hill, into Trinity Square, where stood another place of slaughter, a notable scaffold. That man of peace and prosperity William Penn was born on Tower Hill. Then into Byward Street, where is the church of Allhallows-Barking-by-the-Tower. So called because in its early days it was in the charge of the Abbess of the Benedictine Abbey of Barking in Essex, close by Tilbury. It is one of the City churches that narrowly escaped the Great Fire; the main portion of the edifice is perpendicular, the pillars of the nave being Norman. The brick tower is the solitary specimen of ecclesiastical architecture in London of the time of Oliver Cromwell. Many who suffered upon the scaffold on Tower Hill were buried here, some being moved afterward to happier resting-places. William Penn was baptised here and John Quincy Adams, President of the United States of America, was married here in 1797.

If we are not in a hurry to get home, we will go along Great Tower Street, Eastcheap, and then up Gracechurch Street into Bishopsgate. Eastcheap is thus named to distinguish it from the chepe in the West of the City, Cheapside. "This Eastcheape," says John Stow, that delightful Surveyor of London, "is now a flesh market of butchers there dwelling on both sides of the street: it had sometimes also cooks mixed amongst the butchers, and such others as sold victuals ready dressed of all sorts. For of old time, when friends did meet, and were disposed to be merry, they went not to dine and sup in taverns, but to the cooks, where they called for meat what they liked. . ." We cannot do exactly that, but at the corner of

Fenchurch Street and Mark Lane is the London Tavern, with goodly entertainment. This house stands on the side of the King's Head, where Queen Bess ate her dinner when she was freed from the Tower in 1554.

Also, in George Yard, off Lombard Street—Ask your way!—is the old-world George and Vulture, where both the liquid and solid refreshments are capital and where again you will meet Mr. Pickwick, for that immortal and the equally immortal Sam "took up their present abode in very good, old-fashioned, and comfortable quarters: to wit, the George and Vulture Tavern and Hotel." Mr. P. had two pints "of particular port"; we may have the like quality. But I daresay we shall not be stout enough to tackle the like quantity, for we are degenerate drinkers of Port wine in these days.

Gracechurch Street, which we have crossed to reach Lombard Street, was so called because a church at the corner of Fenchurch Street, dedicated to Saint Benet, was called grass church, a herb market being held adjacent, where was sold corn, malt and so on. There was another grain market on Cornhill close by. Many of these City street names chronicle the social history of London.

Bishopsgate led to (and from) one of the City gates, when London was fortified with walls, bastions, ditches. We have come here, past quaint St. Ethelburgha's, to visit Great Saint Helen's Place, on the right side as we go North, wherein is Saint Helen's Church (PLATE VIII), which came scathless through the Fire. It is said that there was a church here in Saxon times, and who can certainly say "Nay, not so"? Here in 1212 was founded a

Priory of Benedictine nuns, which grew great and wealthy, and to which was attached the church we are visiting. We are in touch with the city of mediæval London, which was a nest of churches and holy houses, many swept away by the Reformation. Stow paints this London, and many scenes of Shakespeare's historical plays were laid in it. To him his English history was vivid and not "ancient" history as it is to us; it was alive, not dead bones. The church was two naves, one having been used by the shy nuns and the other as a Parish church. I will not make an attempt to describe the building; you must see it, as well as you can in "the dim religious light" of the interior. Here are the tombs of many of the City's great, including those of the rich grocer Sir John Crosby, who dwelt close by in Crosby Hall, which figures in Shakespeare's Richard III, and is now rebuilt by the side of the Thames at Chelsea; of Sir Thomas Gresham, builder of the Royal Exchange; and of the quaintly named Sir Julius Cæsar, eminent in the law, with his epitaph on a slab in form of a parchment deed, with seal attached, wherein he says he will "willingly pay the debt of Nature when it might please God to demand it." Did he pay it willingly? Few men do. I do not know any other place in the City in which one gets so fully into touch with the merchant men of old, who did so much for their city and for the commerce of the country.

In London Wall, across Bishopsgate, the little church of All Hallows was built in 1765 by George Dance, designer of old Newgate. Its vestry actually incorporates a bastion of London's Roman wall! In a maze of tall offices lies the

lovely, but little known, nave of the fourteenth century priory church of Austin Friars, a fine piece of flowing Decorated; for over two centuries the place of worship of the Dutch community in London.
It is now high time, probably was so long ago, to be wending our way home.

THIRD TOUR

ROUTE: Trafalgar Square; Haymarket; Piccadilly; Hyde Park; Kensington; Notting Hill; Bayswater; Mayfair; Saint James's Street; Pall Mall; Trafalgar Square.

AGAIN starting from Trafalgar Square, going Westward along the front of the National Gallery, along Pall Mall East, we will turn to the right up the Haymarket. Another name with a story. Until about 1830 a hay market was held here, on Tuesdays, Thursdays and Saturdays. No more do you get the scent o' the hay here, but only the stink of petrol. Immediately on the left, as we go up the street, is His Majesty's Theatre, haunted by the memory of many notable performances by Herbert Beerbohm Tree. Opposite is the famous old house, The Theatre Royal Haymarket, on a site alongside that on which was a playhouse as long ago as 1721. Here you may almost always see a good comedy and quite always admirable acting. Near the top of the street, on the right hand, is an old-world shop-front, "The Old Snuff House of Fribourg and Treyer, at the Sign of the Rasp and Crown, No. 34 Saint James's Haymarket" (PLATE XII), and there it has been since the year 1720! Many men and women, famous and the reverse, have purchased their

PLATE XII

The Old Snuff House
In the Haymarket

Piccadilly
Looking towards Hyde Park Corner

PLATE XIII

ROMNEY'S STUDIO, HOLLY BUSH HILL, HAMPSTEAD

CHURCH ROW, HAMPSTEAD

snuff here, among them the too-much maligned George IV; Mr. Adam, Royal Terrace, Adelphi; Mr. David Garrick; Mr. "Beau" Brummell; John Kemble; Charles Matthews; Mr. D'Israeli, 6 King's Road (now Theobalds Road), father of Ben Dizzy, and le Général the Count d'Orsay à Paris, father of the last of the dandies. Does there meet here o' nights a ghostly club of princes, peers and dandies, exchanging snuff and scandal, mourning over the degeneracy of these snuffless days? The earliest mention of the sale of the seductive cigarette here is 1852, at the price of £3 3s. a thousand.

We now go West and left into Piccadilly Circus, which has lost all its charm and is a centre of pretentious and ugly modernity, including blazing electric signs. Its one attraction for the judicious tourist is the big "Tube" station under the roadway, with a huge circle of shop windows, whence you can travel to all quarters of the town and to far suburbia. We will hasten into Piccadilly (PLATE XII), which also has suffered sadly from the changes that time inevitably brings to all save the cities of the dead. The first part of the street is shops, shops, shops, hotels and restaurants, mostly without any history. On the left, looking rather out of place in this rush, is the church of Saint James, built by Wren in 1684, and long the resort of fashionables, who were or wished to be counted religious. But I like best to think that Mr. Charles Cotton rests here, the friend of Mr. Izaak Walton, whom he helped in the writing of *The Compleat Angler*. Mr. Walton was also a hosier in Fleet Street and Mr. Cotton translated Montaigne's Essays. The wicked Duke of Queensberry, "Old

Q.," sleeps beneath the communion table. Does he dream wicked dreams?

On the opposite side of the way is "Albany," well worth walking through as being one of the most tranquil of London's backwaters. Many notables and notorieties have had "chambers" here, among them Byron; Lytton; Macaulay; Gladstone; "John Oliver Hobbes"; Sir Squire Bancroft.

A little further along is Burlington House, home of learned Societies and of The Royal Academy of Arts, where young men are taught to paint, where there is an exhibition of paintings and sculpture open yearly from May to August, and in the winter usually a far more interesting exhibition of old and new masters.

Then we pass Bond Street, which has been well-named the High Street of Mayfair. Soon we reach the portion of Piccadilly where there are houses on one side only, they facing the Green Park; a range of clubs, great mansions and hotels.

In the past, this part of Piccadilly was in the day-time, especially in the Season, the happiest street in London. There was about it an air of leisurely enjoyment and a freedom from cares, as of men and women who had plenty of time and money to spend on the joyous things of life. Many pairs of well-groomed, high-stepping horses in shining harness. Even a Rolls-Royce cannot compete for good looks with an aristocratic landau, with lordly coachman and sedate footman. The pavement crowded with well-dressed men and women. Hansoms bowling along. Top hats and frock coats. Graciousness and courtesy. But, there, why shed inky tears over that which has gone beyond recall? Let us make the best of what has succeeded it.

There is not much to stay us, so we will on to Hyde Park Corner. Noting Apsley house, at the corner next the Park, where the Duke lived, whose mounted statue rides opposite.

We can now desert the highway, going into "The Park." On summer afternoons in the Season and on Sundays from about twelve to half-past one, the walks and chairs near the Achilles Statue and a bit Westward along the road are thronged with fashionable loungers. This is Church Parade. I had as friend an old man who sat there every Sunday, knowing nobody but seeing everybody.

But for those who visit Hyde Park for its own sweet self's sake the best to do is to walk along the road that skirts the Northern bank of the Serpentine. Early on your way, turn aside to the left to peep into the Dell, a very pretty bit of garden making, where bunnies and sundry birds disport themselves. Of course it is foolish of me, but I am most friendly with the sparrows, perky and chirpy and friendly. A stone at this end of the Serpentine is a memorial of the water-supply granted by King Edward the Confessor to the Abbot of Westminster. We go along the edge of the water, past the island and the boats-for-hire; and so to the bridge, which we will cross. On into the Kensington Road. Turning right, a short way on is the Albert Hall, and inside Kensington Gardens the Albert Memorial, of which nothing good can be said. The Hall is used for concerts, boxing contests, political meetings and other affairs. In winter there are excellent concerts here on Sunday afternoons.

Kensington is a Thackeray quarter. By John Barker's big store, turn left into Young Street, where in a bow-windowed house, No. 16, Thacke-

61

ray wrote "Vanity Fair," "Pendennis," "Esmond" and part of "The Newcomes." Field, in "Yesterdays with Authors," tells how when they were walking along Young Street, Thackeray suddenly halted, saying with semi-seriousness: "Down on your knees, you rogue, for here 'Vanity Fair' was penned; and I will go down with you, for I have a high opinion of that little production myself." Look into Kensington Square where Addison, Steele, and Lady Castlewood resided.

Then back and across High Street, with its restless throng of shoppers, into Palace Green, where in 1862 Thackeray built himself a goodly home, in the Queen Anne style of which he was so fond. It is a pity he did not write the life of that monarch, which he vaguely contemplated. Here he died, quietly sleeping, on Christmas Eve, 1863. The last words he corrected were "and my heart throbbed with an exquisite bliss." Among those who stood by his grave at Kensal Green were Dickens, Millais, John Leech, Anthony Trollope, Browning, Cruikshank.

In pleasantly old-world surroundings, close by, is Kensington Palace. It is a not beautiful hodge-podge, but somehow kindly and familiar, the State apartments possessing a curiously alluring, dingy dignity. A touch of ghostliness too; William the Third and his Queen Mary died here; Queen Anne also, and George II. Queen Victoria was born here; the rooms occupied by her when Princess are shown, and very quaintly early Victorian they seem. There are towering and oppressive Royal portraits. Over all a dim, dusty depression.

Quit this sad abode of uninteresting ghosts,

and go in round by a narrow pathway into Kensington Gardens—to see the sunk garden, with the delicious walks of pleached limes; and then the Banqueting House, or Concert Room, or Orangery, for by each of these names it is called by those who know best! A charming red-brick building designed by Wren and built for Queen Anne. I incline to think it was what used to be called a garden house, used for the preservation during the inclement winter months of warm-clime plants. But what does it matter? It is beautiful, and it is pleasant to linger there, calling up a vision of grand ladies and gallant men in wigs, powder, patches, hoops, periwigs, long skirted coats, all so gay and so debonair; but underneath their finery much the same as we are to-day.

We will now strike across the Broad Walk, which runs from North to South of the Gardens, which by the way were once the private grounds of the Palace. Is there in any other city so delightful a rural spot as this? It is peaceful and restful to stroll beneath the trees—limes, elms, chestnuts—or to lie on the grass in their shade; or to sit on a queer, green, iron armchair, the like of which I have seen nowhere else and which you can occupy the whole day for a few pence. Sit, looking over the Long Water, the early part of the Serpentine, from which it is divided by the bridge; do you know of a town view more beautiful? After our rest and our gossip, we will saunter down the grassy slope, still in the shade of the trees, to the statue of Peter Pan. In these gardens his creator was wont to walk alone o' nights, smoking a meditative pipe, and who shall say that Peter was not by his side, holding his hand and asking questions?

Then toward the bridge, and close on the right
is a shady place, where we may take our luncheon
or tea beneath the trees. I can remember this
place when few folk knew it, and there was a cow
here who kindly afforded a drink of milk to the
thirsty. The sparrows here are very friendly.

Which way now? Across the Bridge, then along
under the tree to the North side of the Gardens,
and then to the right inside the railings to the
Marble Arch; or, if tired or in a hurry, out onto the
Bayswater Road, whence by bus to the same
destination. Then by foot down Park Lane,
turning to the left along Upper Brook Street and
so into Grosvenor Square, Mayfair. Mayfair!
The land of aristocracy, fashion, frivolity, dignity
and now-a-days much impudence. From a guide-
book of 1879 I extract this: "Mayfair—strictly the
immediate neighbourhood of Berkeley-square,
but commonly known as the district lying between
Park-lane, Piccadilly, Bond-street, and Brook-
street, is still, from the society point of view, the
crème de la crème of residential London." There still
lingers here a faint aroma of exclusive aristocratic
mansions, which grows fainter day by day, the
worship of the golden calf having ousted respect
for ancestors.

It is worth noting in this Square a relic of the old
days; the funnel-shaped extinguishers on the iron-
work railings in front of some of the houses, in
which the "runners" put out the links, or torches,
they carried to light the way home of their Lords
and Ladies; home in their sedan chairs; when
London knew not gas-lamps and was more dingy
than it is easy for us to realise. There are still public
houses in West London byways bearing the sign

of "The Two Chairmen." Grosvenor was the latest of the London Squares to be lit by gas. It was in a house here that Doctor Johnson was kept waiting on the pleasure of my Lord Chesterfield. Henry Thrale, the Doctor's brewer friend, died here in 1781; "rich beyond the dreams of avarice" he was, or might have been. It was here that Nelson often came to visit his dear Lady Hamilton. Coming to later times, Mr. W. H. Page lived at No. 6: America's ambassador and most understanding friend of England during the War.

The longest lease here does not run out until 2024! An official description reads prosaically thus: "Laid out about the year 1695. A large oval-shaped area surrounded by thick shrubbery. Very attractively laid out with lawns, hard tennis court, flower beds and some fine trees. Overlooked by large dwelling-houses." In the Spring and Autumn it is really beautiful, typical of the Squares for which London is I believe unique.

If you really wish to go luxuriously shopping, "wend your way" along Brook Street or Grosvenor Street on the East side of the Square, and so to Bond Street. If you do not, either because the spirit does not move you or your purse restrains you, then go along Carlos Place, bearing to the left into Berkeley Square, once the most aristocratic spot in London. Have you not read the Ballads of Jeames of Buckley Square and *The Yellowplush Papers?* No? Do so. Thackeray never wrote anything more entertaining. Once upon a time to say that you lived in or near to Berkeley Square wrote you down a person of the highest *ton.* It is still pleasant on a warm summer or even a misty winter afternoon to loiter here, in the shade of the plane-trees in the garden or along the pavements, thinking of the not so long ago days when the Square resounded with "revelry by night" and day, was thronged with high-born dames and their lordly escorts, and when the air was filled with the noise of champing horses. Perhaps it is a trifle dull now; commercialism has planted its nasty feet here and nearby.

In the shady moonlight we shall meet some very particular ghosts. My Lord Clive, who cut his throat at No. 45. At No. 11 Mr. Horace Walpole dwelt and died. Colley Cibber, capital actor, passable playwright, atrocious poet and improver of Shakespeare, lived at the corner of Bruton Street, No. 20. Charles James Fox was at No. 25. Perhaps we shall meet the spirit of the quaint statue of His Majesty King George III, riding in his Roman habit, which adorned the centre of the garden. At No. 5 is Gunter's, long famous for its ices and wedding cakes. I recall the long string of carriages lined up here on summer days, wherein lolled smart ladies the while superb footmen ministered to their icy desires.

Most memorable to my mind, at No. 21 lived Lady Anne Barnard, who wrote "Auld Robin Gray." On the South side of the Square is Lansdowne House, where lived the Earl of Shelburne, who kindly permitted the British colonies in North America to set up as the United States, he not being in a position to say "Nay." A word of warning: you had best avoid No. 50, which is a haunted house.

Sheridan lived in Bruton Street in his hardest-up days, sadly beset by duns, practically besieged. But we will go along Charles Street, at the South-

West corner of the Square, turn to the left down Queen Street, across Curzon Street into Shepherd Market, still one of the very quaintest odd corners of London. We are taking this turn-aside because it will be exciting to call upon Mrs. Rawdon Crawley, more widely known as Miss Rebecca Sharp, who with her husband the Colonel lived on next to nothing a year at No. 3 Curzon Street, according to the clever identification of the late Mr. Charles Van Noorden, who knew so much about the London of Thackeray and Dickens. Did not Becky give "parties at the little house in Curzon Street," on which occasions "many scores of carriages with blazing lamps blocked up the street to the disgust of No. 200, who could not rest for the thunderous knocking, and of 202, who could not sleep for envy. The gigantic footmen who accompanied the vehicles were too big to be contained in Becky's little hall, and were billeted off in the neighbouring public houses," perhaps in some of those still to be found round the corner.

May Fair, so named after an annual fair held hereabouts, of old called Saint James's Fair. The centre of it was in this Shepherd Market, and extended as far as Tyburn Lane, now more kindly called Park Lane. The fair became so scandalously rowdy that an end was made of it in the reign of George I. All is sedately quiet here now, save for the raucous bellowings of motor horns. No historic interest attaches to Shepherd Market as far as its name is concerned, it being called after a Mr. Shepherd who owned the land upon which it was built. But the name is pretty and there is sometimes something in a name.

Now down White Horse Street into Piccadilly,

where turn left, and so to Albemarle Street, where Robert and James Adam lived a while and died. But to all who love letters, Albemarle Street is most notable because there is the publishing house of John Murray, the first of the line being the friend of Byron (who, by the way, was called Birron by his friends), Tommy Moore, Walter Scott, young Ben Dizzy (with whom he quarrelled severely), Washington Irving, George Borrow and many other literary gents.

Then we will cross into Saint James's Street, which with Pall Mall may be and has been called Clubland:

> "Saint James's Street, of classic fame. . .
>   At dusk, when I am strolling there,
>   Dim forms will rise around me;
>   Lepel flits past me in her chair,—
>   And Congreve's airs astound me!
> And once Nell Gwynne, a frail young sprite
>   Look'd kindly when I met her;
> I shook my head, perhaps,—but quite
>   Forgot to quite forget her."

So sang Frederick Locker-Lampson in *London Lyrics*.

It would give no pleasure to present a list of the famous club houses in this street; their names can be found in the London Directory. But we need not rush along; must pause here and there. Going down, toward the gateway of Saint James's Palace, on the right hand, two or three doors along, is the Devonshire Club, where once was the famously infamous gambling-hell known as Crockford's. Founded by a fishmonger of that name; carried on in a most luxurious and lavish manner, with Ude as *chef* at a salary of £1,200. There was no need then to go to Monte Carlo to drop one's money. Crocky died in 1844, very rich. He was not such a fool as to make a fool of himself by gambling. Also, he was, for what he was, an honest man. I should like to have met the inimitable Count d'Orsay there and watched him winning or losing enormously with the utmost calm. Bernal Osborne wrote of him:—

> "Patting the crest of his well-managed steed,
> Proud of his action, D'Orsay vaunts the breed;
> A coat of chocolate, a vest of snow,
> Well brush'd his whiskers, as his boots below;
> A short-napp'd beaver, prodigal in brim,
> With trousers tightened to a well-turn'd limb;
> O'er play, o'er dress, extends his wide domain,
> And Crockford trembles when he calls a main."

Dandies were not mere clothes' horses in those great days!

White's, said to be the oldest club in London, was a terrible place for gambling, including the laying of monstrous bets on the most absurd issues. Boodle's, a charming eighteenth century front, of which Gibbon was a member, The Thatched House and The Cocoa Tree are others among the older clubs, the last perpetuating the name of a chocolate house where naughty Jacobites hob-nobbed in the time of Queen Anne. There are still a few old-established shops here, such as that of James Lock, the hatter. Modernity in Saint James's Street is a misfit.

On the East side, left hand from Piccadilly, is King Street, where there is little to see but something to think about. It is still a bit old-worldly and sedate. At No. 26, in 1765, a Scotchman named MacCall opened Assembly rooms, which in time developed into the fashionable and highly exclusive Almack's. The dances there were managed by a Committee of Dames of very High Degree, and the "entry" being very difficult to obtain was eagerly sought for by everyone who was anyone and by many who being nobodies longed to be considered somebodies. By 1863 the glory thereof was growing dim and soon became a shadowy memory. Dining succeeded to dancing, under a Mr. Willis. Here met the members of the Society of Dilettanti, who in the first instance patronised the Thatched House Tavern in Saint James's Street. They were amateur lovers and patrons of the fine arts who gathered together to exchange views and reviews. The membership was restricted to fifty, who dined together at regular intervals. In 1889 Willis's Rooms were closed and where are dilettanti now? Who knows? I do not, though perhaps I should do so. It is good to think of those leisured days and nights, when men would meet to discuss the fine arts in a generous and understanding spirit. At a house nearly opposite is "Christie's," where works of art are discussed and bought and sold often at prices which must shock and annoy the souls of artists dead and gone, who had as reward penury and posthumous fame. If you are in town when a great picture sale is on here, go and see it; you will find it interesting, and you will be amused at no cost, if you possess self-restraint!

A few steps farther and we reach Saint James's Square, once most dreadfully exclusive and fashionable, but now so no more. Never, I think, the home of outrageous gaiety, but certainly not so dully respectable as it is to-day. It is a pity that dullness and virtue usually go hand in hand. I should have liked being here when, round and round the railings of the garden, Samuel Johnson and Richard Savage, poet of sorts and riotous man-about-town, walked all one night because they could not afford a lodging and "were not at all depressed by their situation; but in high spirits." I have been there late o' night, but I did not meet them. The Doctor, who had much more fun in him than his friends seem to have recognised, delighted in the rhyme about the "fine young lady of high quality" who would be married to the Duke of Leeds—

> "She shall have all that's fine and fair,
> And the best of silk and satin shall wear;
> And ride in a coach to take the air,
> And have a house in Saint James's Square."

London for those who truly love her is a haunted town, and nowhere else than in Saint James's Square will you meet a more admirable crowd of ghosts revisiting their old quarters, now for most of them so greatly changed. Many of them here I am pleased to greet and they do not object to me very much! Naughty Madam Moll Davis, the dancer; dry John Evelyn, whose diary is so matter-of-fact compared with the lively record of his friend Pepys; William III, who climbs down from his horse in the middle of the Garden and who used to come here to visit the Henry Sidney of de Grammont's memoirs; my Lord Chesterfield, who loved to sit peacefully in his easy chair "by a good fire in Saint James's Square"; the adorable *Belle Stuart*, Duchess of Richmond, whose figure is still displayed upon our copper coins; and Lady Blessington, so gorgeous and so fascinating, who resided with her easy-going lord at No. 10, which has also been honoured by no less than three

71

Prime Ministers, Lord Chatham, Lord Derby and Mr. Gladstone. Do they hold ghostly cabinet meetings and discuss the party politics of to-day? Their comments might well be amusing.

At No. 14 is the London Library, which renders such good service to scholars and students; it was founded in 1841, Carlyle being a moving spirit therein.

No. 20, now given over to commerce, is the finest street house in London of Adam design; it was the town house of the Watkin Williams-Wynn family. Its industrialisation means probably you can manage with a little tact to inspect it. Lichfield House, No. 15, is a fine classic mansion by Wyatt. In War time the Washington Inn occupied the gardens, being a club for American officers.

There is a noise of motor-cars by night and day and Saint James's Square might as well change its name, so greatly has it changed its nature. For better or worse, who shall decide?

Finishing our perambulation of the Square at the South-West corner, we will go into Pall Mall, pronounced Pell Mell. I do not like Pall Mall, which does not matter to anyone save myself. It is so solemn this range of somnolent club houses, with The Athenæum at the South East corner, so learned and literary. It was there that Thackeray and Dickens shook hands after their silly quarrel; there that Anthony Trollope decided that Mrs. Proudie must die. In the War time Pall Mall was not so bad being nearly pitch dark at night, so that to-day faded and yesterdays took its place. Lady Castlemaine of unsaintly memory lodged here. Here Pepys made a night of it at least once, considering the hour of ten dreadfully dissipated!

Here Nell Gwynne lived and died; her abode had a garden wall over-looking Saint James's Park, upon which she leaned and flirted with her Charles, whom she shared with so many, but who, I think, was fonder of her than of any of the others. John Evelyn, of course, was duly shocked at His Majesty's misconduct. Here Gainsborough lodged. Sir Walter Scott visited son-in-law Lockhart at his residence here.

Greatly changed since Mr. John Gay sang:

> "Oh, bear me to the paths of fair Pall Mall,
> Safe are thy pavements, grateful is thy smell!
> At distance rolls along the gilded coach,
> Nor sturdy carmen on thy walks encroach;
> No lets would bar thy ways were chairs deny'd
> The soft supports of laziness and pride;
> Shops breathe perfume, thro' sashes ribbons glow,
> The mutual arms of ladies, and the beau."

Then we cross Waterloo Place, dumping ground of unpleasing statues and memorials; then along Pall Mall East, and "so home" into Trafalgar Square.

FOURTH TOUR

ROUTE: Trafalgar Square; Charing Cross Road; Soho Square; Tottenham Court Road; Regent's Park; The Zoo; Camden Town; Hampstead; Finchley Road; Marylebone Road; Portland Place; Regent Street; Leicester Square; Trafalgar Square.

ONCE again we start from Trafalgar Square. It shall be a fine day, because we have to be out of doors for most of our time, not going anywhere particularly interesting indoors. There are many fine days in London, despite the American and Continental belief that we endure our lives amid perpetual gloom, fogs and rain. I have had friends from the States, and from Germany, who gazed bewildered at our lovely blue sky, exclaiming that this was quite unexpected, and as for heat they peered about for the central heating that caused it! But a truce to frivolity. Seriously, unless you have seen London in a fog, you do not know the town in one of its typical aspects. I am of the few who deplore the departure of the real "pea-souper," wherein you knew where was the roadway by falling off the kerb into the stagnating traffic; when you found lamp-posts by running your nose against them; when in the most familiar places it was no disgrace to lose your way. I can even dimly remember the days (not the nights,

74

only) when you hired a link-boy to light you home.
The fogs we have now are mere mists! But even so
they lend softness to the half-seen and beauty to
ugliness. They make modern Regent Street nearly
bearable!

But I must not loiter in this ridiculous manner;
we have far to go to-day and much to see.

Immediately in front of the National Gallery you
will be able to mount a bus; but your car or a
taxi will be better for to-day's jaunting, for you
may have too much leg-exercise climbing up and
down steep bus stairs. You will kindly take a
bus ticket for Cambridge Circus.

We go along Charing Cross Road, a new and
horribly ugly thoroughfare, where there is not
much to note. After passing the Hippodrome,
where there is usually a jolly musical show, on the
left there are hideous blocks of artizans' dwellings,
built to rehouse those who were turned out of their
homes when in 1887 this street was cut through a
nest of slums and "rookeries." On the right hand,
between Leicester Square Tube station and
Cambridge Circus the shops are chiefly occupied
by dealers in second-hand books, where if you
hunt long and carefully you may now and then
pick up a bargain; chiefly then. In Cambridge
Circus is the handsome Palace Theatre, sad memorial of London's lack of appreciation of music, for
it was set up as a home for the production of
English Opera by Richard D'Oyly Carte of Savoy
Opera fame.

Here descend, turn to the left, so into Greek Street,
home of queer restaurants, some of which provide
excellent food, some of which do not. Along it
Northward into Soho Square, another once-was-a-

centre of very gay fashion, but now, alas, almost entirely commercialised. On the East side, that nearest Charing Cross Road, is the Roman Catholic church of Saint Patrick, which brings a touch of Italy to Soho.

This is one of the oldest London Squares, and in its prime one of the most exciting. The stupid but good-looking Duke of Monmouth, natural and un-natural son of Charles II, lived in a big house on the South side, which was why he selected "Soho" as the password at Sedgemoor in 1685. The origin of the name "Soho" is wrop in mystery and likely to remain so.

Commerce, usually so cruel, has been kind to some of the eighteenth century houses. The dull exterior of the House of Charity hides some of the finest mid-eighteenth century interior decoration. There were famous assembly rooms, for dancing and other less reputable sports, kept here by a Mrs. Cornelys in the last quarter of the eighteenth century, on the ground now occupied by the above named church. But I like this place best because my friend Sir Roger de Coverley was a habitant.

We will now get back to Charing Cross Road and our bus, and go up Tottenham Court Road, home of household furniture of all sorts and conditions, new fashioned and old, beautiful and ugly. Imme-diately on the right is the headquarters of the Y.M.C.A., which during the War was the centre of much splendid activity. On the left, close by Goodge Street Tube station, is Whitefield's taber-nacle, in the churchyard whereof is buried Augustus Toplady, author of "Rock of Ages."

We might dive aside to the left for a moment,

just before getting to the Euston Road, to look at Fitzroy Square. Its sides of Adam houses in marble-cement are effective and dignified, even if a little frowsy in parts.

When we reach Euston Road, we will descend to walk Westward until on the right we arrive at Regent's Park; leaving Great Portland Street station on the left and crossing the road and so into the Park.

Posterity has not been over just to, or appreciative of, the Prince Regent, and we Londoners owe him gratitude for the street and the park that bear his name. It is easy to spend pleasant hours strolling about this Park, which is one of the most beautiful. We may even go boating on the lake. But I have conducted you here to go up the Broad Walk, which runs—why do we speak of a walk as running?—from South to North up the East side of the Park, some three-quarters of a mile. On the right, amid the trees, you will meet the gray American squirrels, who have annexed this part of the Park. They are dear little fellows, and if you do happen to have some nuts about you they will be quite familiar.

Near the top of the walk is the South entrance to the Zoo, as Londoners call the gardens of the Zoological Society of London. These were opened to the public as long ago as 1828, among the beginnings of the collection being the animals from the menagerie in the Tower! It is now for you to decide; if you go into the Zoo you will most decidedly not have time to pursue the rest of our day's Tour. It is up to you.

Crossing the Regent's canal, turning to the left and then to the right we make our way to Chalk

77

Farm station on the Hampstead Tube, where we will book for Hampstead.

But—why "Chalk Farm"? It takes us back to old days, when all hereabouts was fair country, where was Chalcot farm, reduced by popular usage to Chalk Farm, which gave way to the White House tavern and tea-gardens. A hundred years ago or so, and for many years later, London was encircled by tea-gardens, which were frequented on summer evenings and on Sundays by citizens and their wives and children. Now most of them are no more, or are sadly degenerate and towny, save a very few, as we shall see when we reach Hampstead. Chalk Farm was famed as a "meeting" place for "discontented" men to settle "their differences with the pistol, as if gunpowder were the stronger argument, and a steady aim the best logic." Among those who thus disported themselves here were Tommy Moore, most peaceful of poets, and Francis Jeffrey, vitriolic critic. But before a shot was fired, the police stepped in and the affair was "off." Jeffrey had remarked to Moore: "What a beautiful morning it is." To which the poet replied: "Yes, a morning made for better purposes." The party was "conveyed crestfallen to Bow Street," where they were made to promise to be good boys. As late as 1846 Dickens wrote of "the bowers for reading and smoking scattered about the tea-gardens at Chalk Farm." The old tavern has been pulled down these many years and ugly modernity reigns supreme.

When taking your train here be sure that you are going to Hampstead! That is the one drawback to these Tubes, that they occasionally take you to where you have no desire to go.

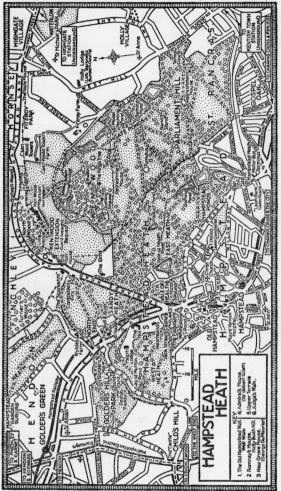

Fig. 15. Plan of Hampstead Heath

If you have set out fairly early, as you should have done, and have not lingered by the way, as you should not have done, you will have time, but not too much, to enjoy yourself at Hampstead. Best not to come on a Saturday or a Sunday, when the crowds are apt to be obtrusive, ruining the atmosphere of quiet which is the chief charm of the Heath.

When the Tube and the lift have landed you on Hampstead Hill, you must resist the temptation to stray about the old and pretty village (PLATE XIII), still for the most part undefiled by modernity, and go down High Street into Downshire Hill, on the left; then to the right into Keats' Grove, where at Wentworth Place, now Lawn Bank, John Keats lived from 1818 to 1820. It is now the Keats Memorial House. In the garden here he may have written the ode "To a Nightingale," and he may not. Not being a lover of museums, if you go in I will await your pleasure outside. When you come out, we will turn to the right, crossing South End Road, and so will find ourselves and may eventually lose ourselves, on East Hampstead Heath. Bearing to the left, going uphill through the Vale of Health (Fig. 15), you will reach the high ground, near the flagstaff, where the Spaniards Road and North End Road join. Opposite is Jack Straw's Castle, a tavern known to all Dickensians and to many others. Dickens wrote to Forster: "You don't feel disposed, do you, to muffle yourself up, and start off with me for a good brisk walk over Hampstead Heath? I know a good 'ous there where we can have a red-hot chop for dinner, and a good glass of wine," which " 'ous" was Jack Straw's Castle. The present building is a couple of hundred years old, or so; there are still red-hot chops and glasses of wine to be obtained; and other things. On a warm afternoon or evening it is quite pleasant to "tea-garden" behind the inn.

However, we have not come here for chops! But to see the view from this highest spot of the Heath. One way you look right over London (PLATE XIV), and on what I may call a half-and-half day it is magnificent. Heavy clouds with bursts of sunshine are the finest "lighting." Right across the grey, smoky town to the Surrey uplands; always with the dome of Saint Paul's as the dominant feature.

> "This is the Heath of Hampstead,
> There is the dome of Saint Paul's;
> Beneath, on the serried house-tops,
> A chequered lustre falls:
>
> And the mighty city of London,
> Under the clouds and the light,
> Seems a low wet beach, half shingle,
> With a few sharp rocks upright."

Thus wrote James Thomson, who would sit here on a Sunday—

> "Too grateful to God for His Sabbath
> To shut its hours in a church."

Looking in the other direction, the "old inhabitant" is plied with regrets, for it is of quite recent years that much peacefully beautiful country has been sacrificed to the red-brick gods of villadom. But still there is a charm in the view; there is a promise in it of free countryside not too far away. But I will allow you to enjoy yourself, uninter-

rupted by the garrulity of an old lover of the Heath
since the days when it could be reached by horse-
power only and seemed to be right outside town.
My advice to you is to be a vagabondish man or
woman here, wandering at your own sweet will.
If you will cast your eye—I always wonder how
that feat is accomplished!—over the map of Hampstead Heath, page 79, you will be able to find
your way about and will find many other places
here of interest which may attract you. I am not
writing a guide-book. But just these two pointers.
It is quite worth while going along the Spaniards
Road, to just about the end of it; in the dip, on the
right hand side, is an old toll-house, shorn of its
gate. If you want to know what-about turnpike
gates read Dickens and other writers of stories
dealing with times about, say, the first quarter
of the nineteenth century. It is a picturesque
corner, this: the quaint gate-house with a background of fine trees; on the other side of the road
that aged hostelry the Spaniards (PLATE XIV). An
interesting house, where you can have a capital
and surprisingly cheap afternoon tea. None of
your twopenny halfpenny cakes, so-called "French
pastries"; but goodly solid bread-and-butter, a
lordly pot of tea, perhaps a lettuce or a plate of
fresh radishes, and jam. I have often eaten too
much here. Why called the Spaniards? I do not
know; nobody knows; lots of people say they know.
The renowned scoundrel Dick Turpin, who was
really a very nasty beast, is said to have been a
frequent visitor here; indeed, he must have been so,
for you will see here preserved his pistols and the
leg-irons which he wore at Newgate while awaiting
his end.

You can walk or bus on to Kenwood, to see its glorious park and Adam house with fine pictures and furniture.

Or you may go down the North End Road, some way along which on the right hand side is the Bull and Bush, which has been more or less rebuilt, unfortunately so from the point of view of the picturesque. Once upon a time this house was the country home of Hogarth, and the story goes that among others who frequented it when it became a tavern were Sir Joshua Reynolds, Davy Garrick, Sterne, Leigh Hunt, Keats, Shelley and Dickens. There are tea-gardens! Did not Mrs. Bardell and party go in a Hampstead "stage" to Jack Straw's Castle, walking on to partake of tea at the Bull and Bush? Was not their innocent merriment rudely broken by Mr. Jackson, "the young man from Dodson and Fogg's"? The rest of this tragic tale can be read, or re-read, by you in the veracious pages of "The Posthumous Papers of the Pickwick Club."

I suggest that we walk on down the North End Road, which in bits is still amazingly rural, until we reach Golders Green, where we will mount an omnibus, booking ourselves for Baker Street station. The ride along the Finchley Road, one of the longest (if not the very longest) streets in London, gives the "tourist" a very good notion of the new Northern suburbs of London; but it is not otherwise striking. The Swiss Cottage tavern is familiar by name to most Londoners, having until recent years been a bus "terminus." At the corner of Saint John's Wood road is Lord's, world headquarters of cricket; opened in 1814 by one Thomas Lord, elsewhere. Is there any much happier way of passing a sunny summer day than sitting here to watch a match?

Then along Park Road, and so to our immediate destination. As showing how my Tours can be adapted to suit your requirements, if you have visited the Zoo, you can come out by the main entrance, turn to the left along the Outer Circle of the Park, and so inside the Park to Baker Street, or outside it to Lord's.

From Baker Street station we will walk or car it Eastward along the Marylebone Road. A pretty name; Saint Mary on the Bourne, or stream, the Tyburn Brook. We soon pass—at least I shall pass, because this form of entertainment gives me the shudders, Madame Tussaud's Waxworks, which was first shown to the public by Madame in the Strand so long ago as the year 1802. It still is "going strong." A little farther on the opposite side of the way is the Parish Church of Saint Marylebone. In the old building, round the corner, which this replaced, Hogarth laid the scene of the Rake's marriage. There Sheridan was married to Miss Linley. In the present church Robert Browning was married to Elizabeth Barrett; and possibly it was here that Mr. Dombey was married, but that Dickens only knows.

On past the Northern end of Harley Street, where and whereabouts the "specialists" do flock together. Then we turn to the right down Park Crescent, and so into Portland Place, a nice, broad and quite uninteresting thoroughfare, save for a few dignified Adam houses. There is a nice series of smaller but more gracious Adam fronts in Mansfield Street, parallel to our direction. And just by, in Queen Anne Street, is Chandos House, a splendid Adam front, complete with fine railings. The huge new British Broadcasting Pile obliterated old Foley house by Wyatt. It used to be so fashionable, and I believe that peers and privy councillors are still to be found lurking here by those who hanker after such society. Past the Langham Hotel, on the left is London's only decent concert-hall, Queen's Hall, where good music is spasmodically offered us. Hard by is Maskelyne's Mysteries, where most amazing things are done and one is taught to discredit the evidence of one's senses. Opposite is the Regent Street Polytechnic, which carries on a very fine educational work. We are now in Regent Street, and, crossing Oxford Circus, will pursue our way down it.

Again, alas for the days that are no more! Regent Street used to be a bit dingy, I daresay, but it was delightful; now it is palatial and might belong to any other up-to-date city. That is my main objection to modernity; it depersonalises everything. Mass production is the beginning of the end of fine art. Regent Street was laid out between the years 1813 and 1820, with the intent to providing a magnificent "*route du roy*" from the Prince Regent's home, Carlton House—now no more—at the bottom of Waterloo Place, to Regent's Park, where was to be built a wonderful house for him, which, however, never was; which may be fortunate, for it might have been a second Brighton Pavilion! One of which is one more than enough. If you have the desire and the time to be very vagabondish, going down the right side of the street, turn right into Prince's Street and so into Hanover Square, which also has been despoiled by the builder and rebuilder. In George Street, running out of the Southern side, is the church of Saint George's, Hanover Square, once famous for famous and fashionable weddings. In mid-Victorian novels it was the ambition of the heroine to be mated in Saint George's and so be assured of living in Society happily ever afterward. It was dedicated to Britain's patron saint out of compliment to stodgy George I, and architecturally it is no more interesting than that monarch, though it has some good Renaissance glass. But think of the great events that have happened within. Here Sir William Hamilton was married to Emma Hart, the lady whom Romney and Nelson immortalised. Much more interesting was the marriage of Disraeli to his guardian angel Mrs. Wyndham Lewis in 1839; of George Eliot to Mr. Cross in 1880, and of Theodore Roosevelt to Edith Carow in 1886. Here in 1814 Shelley "confirmed" his Scotch marriage with Harriet Westbrook. At No. 24 in this street Nathaniel Hawthorne lived for a while in 1855. Tourists to-day will find much that is delightful in his "Our Old Home."

Back to Regent Street per Conduit Street; a history-of-London name, being taken from the Conduit Mead, now obliterated by Bond Street, whence ran one of the ancient conduits that supplied water to old London. Elizabethan sportsmen used to hunt the hare hereabouts. At the corner of this and Mill Street stood the Coach and Horses, from which Mr. Thomas Thurtell set out in a gig on 24th October, 1823, with Mr. William Weare, whom he murdered that night in Gill's Hill Lane, out beyond Elstree. The crime created a very considerable sensation, chiefly because Thurtell and his accomplices after their deed quite enjoyed a meal of pork chops. By contrast, Doctor Johnson was entertained to tea by Bozzy in his rooms here in 1772. In the "Life" is this: "Dr. Johnson went home with me to my lodgings in Conduit-street and drank tea . . ." On the subject of hospitality the great man made this pronouncement: "You are to consider that ancient hospitality, of which we hear so much, was in an uncommercial country, when men, being idle, were glad to be entertained at rich men's tables. But in a commercial country, a busy country, time becomes more precious, and therefore hospitality is not so much valued. No doubt there is still room for a certain degree of it; and a man has a satisfaction in seeing his friends eating and drinking around him." After their tea, they went on to the Pantheon, which is now a wine merchant's establishment, in Oxford Street, not far Eastward of Oxford Circus. But in recalling all this, we must remember also that Regent Street did not then exist, and that the two had not nearly so cleanly or seemly neighbourhoods through which to walk. The names remain, but the places have greatly changed.

We will now cross and go Southward down Regent Street, turning left into Beak Street, wherein the second turning on the right lets us into Golden Square, another of the once-was-fashionables. Here we will not so much turn our thoughts toward those who really lived, as to many children of fiction and to one of probable fact. This last being Ann, de Quincey's poor-girl friend, to whom he bade farewell in Golden Square, near the corner of Sherrard Street, "not wishing to part in the tumult and blaze of Piccadilly."

Prim Colonel Henry Esmond came here to visit General Webb. Mr. Ralph Nickleby resided here, in a house now gone the way of all houses, "a spacious house," brass-plated. Writing in or about 1838 Dickens says of Golden Square "it is not exactly in anybody's way to or from anywhere. It is one of the squares that have been; a quarter of the town that has gone down in the world, and taken to let lodgings. . . It is a great resort of foreigners. . ." which it is still to some extent, but they are chiefly engaged in business, not vocalists and musicians as they were in Ralph Nickleby's time. Neither then nor now was there or is there anything Golden about the Square, which was probably named after its first builder, one Golding. But it may have originally been Gelding. Does it matter? We need not linger here, but go out of it by one of the Southern outlets into Brewer Street. Going to the left we soon find one of the queerest sights in London. Here, within hail of Piccadilly Circus, is an open air market, here and in Berwick Street; barrows laden with fruits, vegetables, fish, meats, garments of all sorts, ironmongery; lit at night by flaring naphtha-lamps; an amusing and almost picturesque sight. Curiously enough, and we will hope not prophetically, the land here used to be called Knaves' Acre. Rupert Street, called after the fiery Rupert of the Rhine, leads to Shaftesbury Avenue, named after the peaceful, philanthropic Earl of that name; dating from 1886 and notable only for its theatres and restaurants.

Crossing it, warily, for the traffic here is heavy and intermittent, we'll go through Wardour Street into Gerrard Street, which has many famous literary connections; but here once again we find

88

the heavy hand of the rebuilder has been ruthless. To most Londoners Gerrard is no more than the name of a Telephone Exchange! But we here come into touch again with Colonel Henry Esmond, for here lived the notorious Lord Mohun, who slew in a duel the Duke of Hamilton, whom Beatrix was to marry. John Dryden lived and died here, as is noted for the passers-by on a Society of Arts tablet. J. T. Smith, in his entertaining "Book for a Rainy Day," notes under date 1787: "Many a time when I had no inclination to go to bed at the dawn of day, I have looked down from my window to see whether the author of the *Sublime and Beautiful* had left his drawing-room, where I had seen that great orator many a night after he had left the House of Commons seated at a table covered with papers, attended by an amanuensis." To-day Mr. Burke would be using a dictating machine and his words would be typed the morrow morn. But Gerrard Street's main claim to immortality, so much of it as bricks and mortar can ever achieve, is that it was the home of the "Literary Club," founded at the Turk's Head at the corner of Greek Street and Old Compton Street, not far away. We can still dine and sup quite passably well in Gerrard Street, but we cannot keep such company: Burke, Goldsmith, Johnson, Boswell, Reynolds, Garrick, Gibbon, Burney! But with increased membership its distinction decreased, and gradually it degenerated into a mere dining club.

Returning to Wardour Street, turning to the left we easily find our way to Leicester Square, about which books might be and have been written. It is a medley of variety theatres and cinemas, of charitable societies and billiard rooms; of propriety and impropriety. It has always possessed a rather motley reputation. It was aforetime called Leicester Fields and was a favourite ground for duellists. The one past-dweller here, with whose shade I should be pleased to shake hands, is Sir Joshua Reynolds, one of the few who fully appreciated and of the very few who rightly understood Goldsmith.

The garden in the centre was laid out by an eccentric financier Baron Albert Grant, being previously, as Edmund Yates describes it, "a howling wilderness, with broken railings, a receptacle for dead cats and every kind of abomination."

The place is strange now to many of us, who remember the great days of "The Empire," now gone, and of "The Alhambra," when both were the home of fine ballet, with admirable music and dancing, and each was a meeting place of a very jolly character. Alas, as is the case with much of central London, cosmopolitan and characterless grandeur has wiped out the light-hearted past. Or is it that we were more light-hearted then, seeing dull things through rosy glasses?

The outlet at the South Eastern corner of the Square, Green Street, is uninteresting, save that it brings us face to face with the statue of Sir Henry Irving, looking up Charing Cross Road and occupying the ground where stood The Old Curiosity Shop, that near Lincoln's Inn Fields not being the real article.

Again we are in Trafalgar Square.

PLATE XIV

THE SPANIARDS, HAMPSTEAD HEATH

HAMPSTEAD HEATH
Looking toward St. Paul's Cathedral

PLATE XV

RIVERFRONT AT LIMEHOUSE
From an etching by Sir Ernest George

GATE OF THE WEST
INDIA IMPORT DOCK

EAST INDIA DOCK
GATE

ROVING AND RIVERING

The Pool of London; Old Swan Stairs; London Bridge;
Jacob's Island; Cherry Garden Stairs; Wapping;
Limehouse; Barges; Greenwich.

So an end to our designed and deliberate Touring.
I hope you have not been misguided? That our
wanderings have been happy? We have seen but a
very small part of London; better it is to see a
little thoroughly than scamper over a lot. We have
come closer to the town than if we had rushed
round merely sight seeking and seeing.

As I have already said, these Tours need not,
probably cannot, be followed precisely, by Londoner or by visitor. You can select such portions
as suit your wishes or as your time permits you to
cover. Your appetite may be for churches and
chapels; or for picture galleries and museums; or
for seeking out the homes and haunts of famous
men and women. Or you may be in London for
a rush business visit, having only the night time
for pleasuring.

If you should have time for more than I have laid
out, why not go roving? Until you are satiated or
satisfied, or compelled to depart?

Perhaps go afloat? Visiting the river below bridge?
The Pool of London is that part of the Thames
River immediately below London Bridge. In the
ordinary sense of the term it cannot be called
beautiful; but it has a picturesqueness of its own for
those who have eyes to see it. Indeed, what river
can be really ugly, however much it is abused by

man? For me the river of London has always been fascinating; by night when it mirrors the myriad lights on bridges and embankments; by day when it ripples sparkling in the sun, or heaves lethargically beneath leaden skies, or runs mysteriously under a pall of swirling fog. Or when it is a gray-white day: mingled sunshine and cold showers. We will set forth in a wherry from Old Swan Stairs, close above London Bridge; but not rowed by such a jolly young waterman as was immortalised by Charles Dibdin:

> "And did you not hear of a jolly young waterman,
>   Who at Blackfriars Bridge used to ply?
> He feathered his oars with such skill and dexterity,
>   Winning each heart and delighting each eye."

We shall be able, after enquiring at one or other of the Thames piers, probably that at Westminster, to secure the services and the boat of a man of great skill and dexterity; who knows every eddy and swirl of the tricky currents and swift tides.

The Pool of London is replete with history and romance. At our starting place, most suitably the Old Swan Stairs, Shakespeare and his fellow players must often have embarked and disembarked; many other famous wights also. "Stairs" were—and are—steps leading down from the river bank to the water's edge, for the convenience of those taking boats.

Looking across the water, we see the dim, dingy outline of the wharves and warehouses upon Bankside, where in Elizabethan days were the Globe and Swan playhouses, the Bear Garden, where bears were cruelly maltreated by huge dogs and still more savage men, and other places of entertainment, seemly and otherwise. There, too, is the stalwart square tower of Saint Saviour's, Southwark.

We pass beneath London Bridge: first built in stone between the years 1176 and 1209; rebuilt in 1825-1831. In olden days it was one of the wonders of the world, with its gallant rows of wooden houses on either side of the roadway, a chapel dedicated to Saint Thomas à Becket and a fortified gatehouse which was usually adorned with the mouldering skulls of unsuccessful rebels and other rash persons. To-day it is just a gray-stone bridge of no particular impressiveness, but always busy, day and night.

Now we are drifting downstream on the waters of the Pool. On our left hand is Billingsgate, the great fish market of London. For many centuries the wharf here has been busy with fishing boats, English and foreign, including always at least one Dutch eel-ship allowed to anchor here since Queen Elizabeth gave special permission. Then we float, for we should go leisurely on our way, past the Custom House, a huge, cold, classic pile, of not much interest save from the merchants' point of view, and so to the Tower:

"... London's lasting shame,
With many a foul and midnight murder fed."

We will turn our backs upon history, looking across to a place made famous by fiction. That muddy, desolate inlet there leads up to Jacob's Island, where Bill Sikes met his end. It is thus described by Dickens: "Near to that part of the Thames on which the church of Rotherhithe abuts, where the buildings on the banks are dirtiest and the vessels on the river blackest with the dust of colliers and the smoke of close-built low-roofed houses, there

93

exists . . . the filthiest, the strangest, the most extraordinary of the many localities that are hidden in London . . . Jacob's Island, surrounded by a muddy ditch six or eight feet deep and fifteen or twenty wide when the tide is in . . ." As seen at low tide the massy bank of black, slimy mud looks strangely silver-toned under white, sunlit clouds.

Some little way lower down is a more cheery spot, Cherry Garden Stairs, nearby which, in the days of merry King Charles II, was a well-known place of entertainment, visited among other gay folk by Master Samuel Pepys, who entered in his Diary under date 15th June, 1664, this: "To the Cherry Garden, and then by water singing finely to the Bridge," meaning London Bridge. Fancy that! These gay companions, be-laced and be-plumed, singing as they were rowed homeward. In those days the Thames was the busiest highway in the City, and the brightest, and by a long way the cleanest; crowded with boats and galleys and often the scene of pompous pageantry. Now it is deserted by all save those who have business upon its waters.

A little lower down, on the opposite shore, is Wapping; still "chiefly inhabited by seafaring men and tradesmen dealing in commodities for the supply of shipping and shipmen." It is not a neighbourhood in which you would expect to fall on any trace of romance; nor would one so do but that songs have put its name upon the lips of thousands:

> "Your Molly has never been false she declares,
>   Since last time we parted at Old Wapping Stairs,"

but we have only the lady's word for it. Dibbin sang of another Wapping beauty:

94

"Your London girls, with all their airs,
Must strike to Poll of Wapping Stairs,
    No tighter lass is going.

   .   .   .   .   .

Her father, he's a hearty dog,
Poll makes his flip, and serves his grog,
    And never stints his measure;
She minds full well the house affairs,
She seldom drinks, and never swears;
    And isn't that a pleasure?"

Surely so; but is not a sad slur cast upon the manners of the other maidens of Wapping? Grog is usually rum and water, and was introduced into the navy in the year 1745, or thereabouts, by Admiral Vernon, who was nicknamed "Old Grog" from his habit of wearing a *Grog*ram cloak! There are various kinds of "flips," into the compoundings of which enter ale, spirits, eggs, butter, sugar and spices!

Hereabouts there are some old, wooden, bow-windowed houses, leaning, apparently perilously, over the water; such, for example, as The Prospect of Whitby Inn. There are many of these quaint waterside taverns in this neighbourhood: in Wapping, Shadwell and Limehouse. Best known of them is The Grapes at the last named place, for it has been identified as The Six Jolly Fellowship-Porters in "Our Mutual Friend," wherein Gaffer Hexam, Rogue Riderhood and others disported themselves under the stern eyes of Miss Abbey Potterson; indulging in such giddy drinks as Dog's Nose, Purl, and Flip, doubtless such as Poll made for her father.

And what is Dog's Nose? It was a potent mixture made of beer and gin. There were—indeed are— two kinds of Purl, one concocted of beer or ale and

95

wormwood, and the other of beer and hot spiced gin! No wonder the porters were jolly!

We are told that The Six Jolly Fellowship-Porters was a tavern "of a dropsical appearance . . . a narrow lopsided wooden jumble of corpulent windows heaped one upon another as you might heap as many toppling oranges, with a crazy wooden veranda impending over the water." And "the bar . . . was a bar to soften the human breast," and apparently to make jolly the hearts of porters and others fond of good fellowship. Those who know their way about this town can still find in this and in other parts old-fashioned taverns; cosy places where there are good cheer and cheery faces to be enjoyed.

It may not be out of place to mention that the Fellowship-Porters formed one of the London guilds or brotherhoods, the members claiming and until recent years retaining the right of unloading all vessels laden with grain that came into the port of London.

One of the busiest parts of the Pool of London is undoubtedly Limehouse (PLATE xv). Here huge warehouses open wide their doors for the reception of merchandise from all over the world. Although the great majority of these warehouses are modern, there are still a number of the quaint old-fashioned buildings along the water front containing dark, poky little dens where in former years men lingered, like Dan Chaucer, "over bills of lading."

There was also at a much later period that strange conglomeration of ship wreckage and marine stores surrounding a dilapidated shed of an office, such as Dickens describes as Quilp's Wharf, in his story of the "Old Curiosity Shop."

Now we turn homeward. We sit lazily; smoking, dreaming. The sky is a pageant of gray and white clouds sweeping across the blue; the sun shines bravely between bitter showers. All around is the turmoil of the busy seaport.

One of the most picturesque types of craft in the world is the Thames barge. In its various forms it has figured in the history of the river from time immemorial. It was in barges of a glorified type that royalty used to be conveyed in the days when the river was the main highway of the state processions of all descriptions.

A barge, with huge tan-coloured sail, goes slowly by; how much more dignity there than in the fussy motor boat that races past! When I was a tiny little boy it was always my ambition to live upon a barge, and indeed there are worse lives to be led! Even nowadays I have a hankering that way, believing that I could be very happy so, going placidly about the waterways of old England.

So back to Old Swan Stairs.

Or you may go down stream by steamer or electric launch to Greenwich, on the right passing Deptford, where in 1581 Queen Bess dined on board the *Golden Hind,* in which Captain Francis Drake had made his trip round the world; afterward knighting her gallant host. In the churchyard of Saint Nicholas, is buried Christopher Marlowe, concerning whose death so many fables have been invented.

A little farther on is Greenwich, still beautiful, but not nearly so pleasant a good many years since when we went down there on a "penny" steamer on summer afternoons; for a fish dinner at the *Trafalgar* or the *Ship*; sitting afterward on the grass plot, looking over the broad, busy river and watching the sunset behind the London smoke.

> "We feasted full on every famous dish,
>   Dress'd many ways, of sea and river fish—
> Perch, mullet, eels, and salmon, all were there,
> And whitebait, daintiest of our fishy fare."

I should have enjoyed being there on 24th July, 1848, when Macready, the actor-manager, and some American friends jaunted to Greenwich, being joined in the evening at the *Trafalgar* by Mr. and Mrs. Charles Dickens, her sister Miss Hogarth, Stanfield and Maclise, the painters, and a few more: "We sat down to one of those peculiar English banquets, a whitebait-dinner. We were all very cheerful—very gay; all unbent, and without ever forgetting the respect due to each other; all was mirth unrestrained and delighted gaiety. Songs were sung in rapid succession, and jests flung about from each part of the table. Choruses broke out, and the reins were flung over the necks of the merry set. After 'Auld Lang Syne' sung by all . . . we returned home in our hired carriage, and an omnibus hired for the nonce. . . A very happy day." There now; how giddy yet respectful. Very Macreadyish!

There is the hospital to visit, but I should prefer, if we could, to see the Tudor Palace which occupied this same site, where Elizabeth was born, and as Queen spent many of her days with much pomp and circumstance. Better worth seeing is the Park, which was laid out by good King Charles II. The view from the high ground over London and the river is splendid. I am compelled to quote Boswell: "On Saturday, July 30 (1763), Dr. Johnson and I took a sculler at the Temple-stairs, and set out for Greenwich. . . We landed at the Old Swan,* and walked to Billingsgate, where we took oars and moved smoothly along the silver Thames. It was a very fine day. We were entertained with the immense number and variety of ships that were lying at anchor, and with the beautiful country on each side of the river. . . I was much pleased to find myself with Johnson at Greenwich, which he celebrates in his 'London' as a favourite scene. I had the poem in my pocket, and read the lines aloud with enthusiasm:

> 'On Thames's banks in silent thought we stood,
> Where Greenwich smiles upon the silver flood:
> Pleas'd with the seat that gave ELIZA birth,
> We kneel, and kiss the consecrated earth.'

He remarked that the structure of Greenwich hospital was too magnificent for a place of charity, and that its parts were too much detached to make a great whole. . . We walked in the evening in Greenwich Park. He asked me, I suppose, by way of trying my disposition, 'Is not this very fine?' Having no exquisite relish of the beauties of Nature, and being more delighted with 'the busy hum of men,' I answered, 'Yes, Sir; but not equal to Fleet-street.' JOHNSON: 'You are right, Sir.' " They wound up the day "very socially" at the Turk's Head coffee-house in the Strand.

So, farewell to the River, and we, too, must say "Farewell," for this is the end of TOURING LONDON.

*This to escape the dangerous "shooting" of London Bridge.

FIG. 16. ST. BENETS', PAUL'S WHARF

A Wren Church with Welsh services

A BRIEF INDEX

NOTE: *This is not a full Index, which would serve no useful purpose, but is a guide for the enquiring London "Tourist."*

NOTES

NOTES

NOTES

NOTES

NOTES

NOTES